EVERYDAY NUMEROLOGY

Yearly Planning Made Easy

ALSO BY PAULINE EDWARD

Gateway to a New World

Aquarius: The Age of Revelation, Choice and Transformation

The Healing of Humanity

The Movement of Being

Choosing the Miracle

Leaving the Desert: Embracing the Simplicity of A Course in Miracles

Making Peace with God: The Journey of a Course in Miracles Student

Astrological Crosses: Exploring the Cardinal, Fixed and Mutable Modes

L'Hermès: Dictionnaire des correspondances symboliques, with Marc Bériault and Axel Harvey

EVERYDAY NUMEROLOGY

Yearly Planning Made Easy

Pauline Edward

Copyright © 2025 Pauline Edward

Published by Pauline Edward, Montreal, Canada

All rights reserved. No part of this work may be reproduced or used in any form or by any means, electronic, digital, or mechanical, including photocopying, recording, or any retrieval system, without the prior written permission of the publisher.

Paperback ISBN 978-1-927694-10-7
Hardcover ISBN 978-1-927694-18-3

Cover design, graphics, and layout: Pauline Edward

Contents

Preface vii
Introduction xi
1. Introducing the Numbers 1
2. Your Personal Life Roadmap 33
3. The 9-Year Epicycle 57
4. The 1 Personal Year 75
5. The 2 Personal Year 89
6. The 3 Personal Year 105
7. The 4 Personal Year 119
8. The 5 Personal Year 133
9. The 6 Personal Year 145
10. The 7 Personal Year 159
11. The 8 Personal Year 171
12. The 9 Personal Year 183
13. The Pinnacle Numbers 197
14. Putting It All Together 213
Bibliography 227
About the Author 228

Preface

Everyday Numerology is an updated version of *The Power of Time: Understanding the Cycles of Your Life's Path*, originally published in 2007 by Llewellyn Publications. The purpose of this book is to facilitate yearly planning, something that is very much needed in these hectic times. In a complete study of numerology, the numbers from the Birth Name, current name, nicknames, and numbers linking the Birth Date and name numbers would be used. Although a fascinating study in its complete form, many people would feel overwhelmed if faced with the prospect of analyzing and interpreting twenty to thirty number values.

This book was written for those who spend valuable time planning and goal setting, both professionally and personally, and want to know more about the natural cycles at work in their lives. Most of these people have careers as well as family responsibilities, and simply don't have the time or the inclination to undertake the years of study normally required for the mastery of numerology.

Everyday Numerology therefore focuses on the numbers derived from the date of birth not only because they are simple to calculate and easy to learn, but also because they clearly reveal the path of your life, like a roadmap you might use for direction on a long journey. A large part of this book is devoted to the Personal Year number, probably the single most powerful tool for planning and goal setting. Exercises have been included throughout to help you easily integrate and apply the information. As you discover the natural cycles and trends at work through your numbers, much of the pressure and anxiety that normally exists when steering the ship of your life into uncharted waters will fade. Instead, you will move forward with more understanding, confidence, and joy.

A simple introduction to the name numbers has been included in the last chapter, along with a brief look at the Lunar Cycle and Mercury Retrograde. Why not have a little fun on this journey! Plus, being informed will make it so much smoother.

Who Might Enjoy This Book?

This book is for those who are curious about the meaning of the numbers and how this might be applied in their everyday lives. The approach is practical and hands-on, and especially very easy to use for the person with a hectic lifestyle. Given the powerful system of knowledge contained in the numbers, everyone who wants a clearer sense of direction should read this book. This book is for you if:

- You are intimidated by numbers and would appreciate a simplified introduction to numerology.
- You have absolutely no knowledge of numerology.
- You have an interest, but not the time for an extensive study.
- You have some knowledge or experience with numerology and would like to know more.
- You wouldn't be caught dead consulting a numerologist, but your curiosity got the better of you.
- You'll try anything once.
- A friend recommended this book, and now your curiosity is piqued.
- You don't believe in anything that can't be scientifically proven, so you've decided to prove that numbers don't work, although unconsciously, a part of you secretly hopes to find some measure of truth.

But mostly, this book is for you if:

- You need to clarify your life purpose and get back on track.

PREFACE

- You are ready to unlock some of your hidden talents and skills.
- You want to have a better sense of control.
- You want to set and achieve exciting new goals for yourself or your business.
- You have some decisions to make and don't know where to turn.
- You have a busy schedule and want to make the best use of your time.
- You want to be certain to take advantage of your opportunities at the right time.
- You seek a better understanding of the forces at work in the lives of the people close to you.
- You are at a crossroads and ready to make a fresh new start.

By reading this book, you will:

- Gain a deeper understanding of your life purpose.
- Learn how to sort out what is important for you from what is not.
- Learn how to focus on your needs and opportunities given your unique trends and timeframe.
- Learn how to make your action plans even more effective.
- Identify and learn how to deal with potential obstacles.
- Gain the knowledge and confidence you need to achieve your goals and live a rich and fulfilling life.

Above all, you will feel much more in alignment with your natural cycles and will experience increased inner harmony, peace, confidence, greater success, and an overall sense of purpose and satisfaction. This book will very likely change the way you plan for your future!

Fun with Numbers

Are you a 1? Focus on you but don't forget others.
Which brings us to 2, who's quite sensitive to others.
3 is for fun and creativity.
But need to have that stable 4 where family, work, and health are key.
5 adds that extra leg to the chair and brings innovation and experimentation.
6 finds responsibility, harmony, and healing; what a creation!
7 looks inward but seeks Higher Answers and Self.
8 is the height of success, vision, and accomplishment. Put that trophy on your shelf!
While 9 brings completion, rest, and the Big Picture.
What numbers speak to you?
We can relate to all of them.
Read Pauline's book to see your unique number vibration,
And plan for your future iteration!

Michael J. Miller

A huge thank you to Epp, Sherry, and E'mya for your encouragement, feedback, and help with the edits of this book. And of course, a huge thank you to Michael Miller. With his Life Path 8, in a Personal Year 8, and Personal Month 8, he officially earned the title of CEO, that is, Chief Editing Officer. And yes, numbers can be fun. You can count on it! Thank you!!!

Introduction

Numerology came into my life in 1994, which, for me, was just at the right time. The knowledge I gained helped clarify why my life was in such turmoil, why things weren't going the way I wanted them to, and, more importantly, what I could do to set myself on a healthier course for the future. Having studied and practised astrology for over two decades, I already had a good sense of my life purpose, but somehow circumstances had piled up and I felt as though I had temporarily lost my way. Numerology provided me with a fresh new angle on my situation, shedding light on a state of affairs that at the time seemed insurmountable, giving me not only the hope, but also the knowledge and understanding I needed to get back on track.

After integrating numerology into my practice, many of my clients were quite eager to learn about the cycles at work in their lives. Numerology is much easier to learn and use than astrology; an exact time of birth is not required and calculations are limited to simple sums and subtractions. This book was written for those who would like to incorporate some of the basic principles of numerology to clarify their life's journey and improve their planning and goal setting.

The Best Laid Plans…

It's not uncommon to find ourselves participating in conversations that centre on how hectic the pace of life has become. This is even truer today than it was when the first edition of this book was written. We share how overwhelmed we feel, how we struggle to find—never mind maintain—a balance between our personal and professional lives. By the looks of it, this trend isn't likely to abate any time soon, and may very well continue to grow! Despite our concerns, it would appear that we are far more resilient and adaptable than we might have imagined, for the more curves get thrown at us, the more we appear to cope. Nonetheless, judging by the growing number of people suffering from anxiety, sleeplessness, burnouts, confusion, and other stress-related conditions, it would appear that our coping mechanisms could use a little help.

And help abounds! Bookstores, the Internet, and social media promise solutions for all aspects of our lives from physical, mental, emotional, relational, and spiritual to financial. We're learning about work-life wellness, balance, the importance of self-care, making better choices, creating effective habits, living with purpose, effective goal-setting, the importance of visualization, the relationship between job satisfaction and health, manifesting with intention, love and relationships, longevity, productivity, the shift in consciousness,… the list is endless. We're applying all manner of clever plans, systems, approaches, and methods. Compared to fifty years ago, we have an astounding, perhaps even overwhelming, abundance of resources available today.

To top it all off, we seem to be living in an ever-expanding trend of self-accountability and empowerment. We are encouraged to become responsible for the outcome of our lives. Our success, we are told, is the result of not only our talents and abilities, but also of our thought patterns, our belief systems, and our ability to focus on our goals. The pressure mounts. We are taught to visualize with intention, to create the future we wish to experience. Our future lies in our hands. If we aren't reaching our goals, we must be doing something wrong, we aren't working hard enough, or we don't believe in our goals or in ourselves enough. For many people, gone are the days of blaming parents, schooling, the economy, politics, and society for their defects and woes. *Your* decisions, *your* actions, *your* power, *your* results, *your* responsibility, *your* fault. Faced with the heavy burden of

INTRODUCTION

responsibility for their own success, some people never leave the starting gate, fearful of possible failure should they commit to entering the race.

Suppose you've been applying yourself diligently at uncovering your life purpose and developing healthy new habits. You've hired a coach. You have a support team. You've read the books and produced what you think is a dynamite, fail-proof plan. You've worked on your attitude and your mindset; you're motivated. You diligently write your affirmations and practise visualizing your intentions. You're focused. Yet, despite the best-laid plans of man and mentor, unforeseen circumstances arise and trends change, getting in the way of your progress and eventually diminishing your feelings of satisfaction. Your confidence begins to falter. You wonder where you went wrong. You can't seem to get it right. Why are you not making the progress you expected in the timeframe you had so painstakingly determined?

Here's a good question: Have you ever stopped long enough to ask yourself whether or not you were applying the correct methods at the correct *time*? Not in terms of market trends, seasons, or any other external factor, but the right time for *you*, in terms of your own natural cycles. Would you expect to harvest tomatoes from a seedling planted in the middle of a January frost? Of course not. No matter how good a gardener you are, it just wouldn't work. Rather than arbitrarily establishing deadlines and target dates for attaining personal, career, business, and financial goals with no valid sense of whether or not the timing is right, imagine if you could establish a real timeline, one that made sense and was in alignment with your personal seasons. Imagine the power and effectiveness of such a working tool! By reading this book, you will become aware of some very powerful natural cycles at work in your life through the set of numbers that are derived from your date of birth. What better test of a system of knowledge than to experience it directly in your life?

On Predicting the Future

Some people take offence at the idea that events can in some way be predetermined or that they can be forecasted. They fear that if they consult astrology or numerology they will be influenced and may lose the precious freedom to make their own choices. *Why consult the stars? They ask. I know where I'm going, what more will it give me? I don't believe in destiny; I'd rather determine my own future. I don't want anyone to influence my decisions.* These are indeed legitimate questions and objections.

While searching for an interesting and effective way to respond to these objections, an avid golfer pointed out that the game of golf was a metaphor for life. Intrigued, I did a little digging and found a way to explain how I use astrology and numerology. My research led me to discover that golf is a complex and fascinating sport. It has rules, dress codes, social protocol, business etiquette, environmental issues (to spray or not to spray), and Zen-like attributes (stillness, focus, presence). No wonder so many people get hooked! Most golf courses, I learned, provide a card with a map. There are also pins marking the locations of the holes. So, while you keep your eye on the ball, you have a general idea of the terrain you must cover and a clear picture of where you are going.

Now, does the fact that you have consulted the map predict how well or how poorly you will play? Because you are aware of the layout of the course and have focused on the pins, has the outcome of your game been predetermined? Is your freedom to play your best game diminished? The answer to all these questions is a resounding no. The fact of the matter is that having consulted the map helps you focus your attention on your game, lets you concentrate on your swing, and most likely improves your chances of a favourable outcome.

Everyone will agree that in the end, practice, skill, training, and mindset will determine the outcome of your game, and not the map or the pins. Maps are there to indicate direction, terrain, potential obstacles, and distance. They enable you to create

INTRODUCTION

an effective plan, determine time and measures, and choose the route that is most suitable for your needs, abilities, and goals. Would you play golf without a map or pins? You could, but with no idea of the layout of the course, it might take you a very long time to complete eighteen holes. Now I ask, why live your life without a map?

You don't have a map? Actually, you do. As we will see, the numbers derived from your date of birth provide you with the map and the pins of the course of your life. They reveal information about the layout of your journey, indicating the bumps, obstacles, twists and turns, opportunities, timings, trends, and tendencies. You remain free to play out your game as you choose. A good map simply helps you play your best game.

There is in fact a vast difference between being foretold the details of your future and having a practical sense of trends to come. It's much like when you consult the weather network for the upcoming weekend forecast. The weatherman checks weather maps and patterns and interprets the data in a way that we can understand. A low-pressure system will likely bring warmer temperatures and the possibility of rain; a cold front might indicate a sunny day. We take this information and plan our activities accordingly. Yet at no point does the weatherman actually tell you or determine what you will do on that rainy or sunny day. You are simply given information based on data that has been gathered through tests and measurements. You remain free to make decisions about what you will or will not do on that particular day. You also accept that there is nothing you can do about the forecasted weather system. However, while you can't change the weather pattern to one that is more suitable for your desires or needs, you can choose what you will do.

A similar situation applies when you consult an astrologer or numerologist, who is in many ways like the weatherman describing upcoming climate and weather trends. Only in this case, you are being shown your personal weather patterns. You still remain free to decide what you will do given your trends, but there is little you can do about the trends themselves. In this book, you will learn to identify your upcoming trends with sufficient accuracy and detail so you can make better choices, based on your personal journey. You will in effect become the captain of the ship of your life rather than a passive passenger, subject to the tides of the future.

The Numbers Used in This Book

In this book, we will examine the main numbers derived from the Birth Date. Besides being easy to work with, this basic set of numbers effectively maps out the entire course of a person's life, facilitating short-term and long-term planning and goal setting. As mentioned in the Preface, to add a little extra insight, we will take a brief look at the numbers derived from your name.

In addition to a study of the cycles and their trends, you will find exercises along with tips and suggestions for making the most of your personal cycles. Sometimes when you're in the thick of it, it can be difficult to be objective and to come up with creative solutions. The "My Experience of the Numbers" exercise in Chapter 1 will provide you with a good, basic introduction to the impact of the numbers in your life. The goal of this book is to provide a framework, and some helpful and even fun ideas for making your journey all the more productive and certainly more enjoyable.

A complete study of the numbers and related cycles is not only beyond the scope of this book, but also not its intended purpose. If you should experience a period that seems particularly unclear or challenging, you might consider consulting a professional numerologist. An objective perspective on what appears to be a complex or difficult situation might help you obtain the clarity you need to get back on track.

INTRODUCTION

How to Use this Book

You are no doubt eager to learn what the numbers hold in store for you. This book has been organized in such a way as to provide you with maximum benefits in the shortest amount of time. By completing a few preliminary steps, you'll be ready to design a super plan for your future.

1. Chapter 1 introduces the numbers. Complete the "My Experience of the Numbers" exercise. By acquainting yourself with the language of the numbers, it will be easier for you to understand the role they play in your life.

2. Next, sharpen your pencils. In Chapter 2, we begin with the calculation of the Life Path number. Complete the "Where Am I Now?" exercise.

3. Chapter 3 introduces the important Personal Year number. You are no doubt eager to move ahead and find out what your year holds for you. Take the time to complete the "Key Life Sectors" and "My Personal History" exercises. They will improve your ability to plan effectively and provide you with deeper insights as to how the numbers work in your life.

4. Chapters 4 to 12 provide an in-depth description of each of the nine Personal Years. Complete the two exercises associated with your current Personal Year found at the end of each chapter. Use this information to set goals that are appropriate for you, based on your personal cycles.

5. For a broader picture of your life journey, in Chapter 13 you will add the Pinnacle numbers to your roadmap.

6. In chapter 14, you will put all your numbers together in handy reference charts. This will give you a clearer perspective on where you are and where you are going.

7. Understandably, once you have completed the basic calculations, you will want to jump ahead to the chapter that

pertains to your current Personal Year. By all means do so, but for added benefits, afterward do read the sections on all the Personal Years. With a complete picture of the 9-Year Epicycle, you will make more effective plans, and maybe even manage to work in an extended vacation in your next number 9 Personal Year.

If you become hooked on the numbers and like to use your daily numbers when planning activities, there is a PDF on the Calculations page on my website (www.paulineedward.com) that includes daily numbers calculated for each personal year. It's free to download.

Planning and goal setting need not be arduous chores. Within the context of your current situation, use your creativity and imagination to take full advantage of the energies at work in your life. Most of all, remember to have fun with your numbers!

CHAPTER 1
Introducing the Numbers

There's no hiding from numbers. We deal with them on a daily basis; from the moment we wake up in the morning and strain an eye to read the digital clock, until we check how many messages we missed on our phone before going to bed. The study of numbers has captivated humanity for millennia, and can be found in every discipline, including mathematics and science, art and music, the occult, and most religious and spiritual practices. Today, a growing number of entrepreneurs, managers, and other highly educated people are using numerology to plan their lives. Foolish and superstitious people you might say? But, what if numerology really *can* give you the inside edge?

How does numerology work? The fact is that we don't know exactly how it works, only that hundreds of years of study, practice, and observation show that it does. Note that apples fell from trees long before Newton discovered the law of gravity, and numerology will continue to work until science discovers more of the mysteries of the universe. In the meantime, why not use this amazing body of knowledge to our advantage?

Numbers are everywhere. Some people have a favourite number, a lucky number, or even an unlucky number; others are completely intimidated by numbers. Today, everyone has secret numbers such as PINs, codes, and passwords. A client of mine became very excited when I mentioned the age of 57 as an important turning point in his life's journey. For many years, the number 57 had been a recurring theme. Whenever 57 appeared on a bill, address, or telephone number, for example, he saw significance in that moment. The age of 57, I explained, was the most likely age for his retirement rather than the age of 55, as he had originally planned, since 57 corresponded to the end of one of his numerology cycles. The end of a cycle often manifests as the end of a period of activity, such as a job, relationship, career, or project. Months later, Ken informed me that revised financial projections and the state of the economy had caused him to readjust his plans. He was right on track for reaching his retirement goals at the age of 57, the beginning of a new phase of his journey.

Like many entrepreneurs, Ken was very intuitive. Without knowing anything about numerology, he had tapped into an important turning point in his cycles. In his case, it had shown up in seemingly incidental ways. Many people have a sense of their timings without being aware of their numerology cycles. It was not uncommon for clients to express surprise when I pointed out upcoming turning points from their charts. "I've always had a feeling that such and such would happen when I reached forty-two," they might say.

For example, you might have sensed, intuitively, at some key point in your life that it was time to do something in particular. Maybe you followed a hunch and introduced yourself to a certain person who later provided important opportunities for you, or you applied for the position you wanted *just at the right time*, or you signed up for a particular course in college that *just happened to turn your life around*. Some people don't listen to their inner voice. You know these people. They are the ones who are always complaining about their rotten luck. They are the ones who say, "I should have done it when the timing was right, but I didn't listen to myself."

If you had been aware of your numerology cycles, you would not have found anything unusual about your decision and its accidental result. Numerology clearly shows your trends and their most likely outcomes. By the same token, given the force of the cycles and trends at work in our lives, no matter how hard

CHAPTER 1 • INTRODUCING THE NUMBERS

you may wish for something, if it's not the right time, it simply is not the right time. Those are the times when, no matter how hard you try, things just don't seem to work. You won't grow tomatoes if you plant them in the middle of a January frost. Yet, although you can't cheat your cycles, you can work with them and take advantage of the opportunities they present, for every moment holds an opportunity.

There Is a Time for Everything

From birth to death we encounter the energies of countless cycles—some internal, others external—from our biological cycles to the four seasons, to the cycles of economics, finance, real estate, and politics. We are exposed to trends in the arts, social media, marketing, and fashion, as well as health, diet, self-help, and spirituality. Yet, despite all these common influences, how is it that your best friend is falling in love and you're not? Or your colleague got the promotion and you didn't? Your co-worker broke the monthly sales target and you had your worst month ever? Your neighbour is vacationing in the Bahamas while you have to stay home to deal with a broken water main?

Although we all experience many of the same cycles and seasons, no one expects our lives to follow the exact same course. Each of us has a unique set of rhythms and timings, the nature of which, as you will soon discover, is revealed by the numbers derived from the date of birth. Once you become familiar with these numbers, the patterns of your life will take on a whole new meaning. You will have a better understanding of why things happened the way they did, how you got yourself into your current situation, and what to expect in the years to come. The cycles of numerology will help clarify your direction and strengthen your purpose.

Numerology is essentially the practice of assigning numeric values to dates as well as to the names of people, places, and objects. This book focuses on exploring the world of knowledge that resides in the numbers that are derived from your date of birth. These numbers reveal the roadmap of your life, portraying its twists and turns, obstacles and challenges, adventures and opportunities. Other than a quick peek at the name numbers in Chapter 14, these are the numbers we will focus on in this book.

Once you understand the basics, you will find that numbers are fun and easy to work with, and the techniques for using them are straightforward. Your numbers act as signposts, indicating not only the start and end of specific periods, but also the qualities or traits of those periods. Some years are more favourable for growth and expansion. At other times, you would do better by being receptive and flexible rather than active and adventurous. Certain years are great for career advancement, while others are best for dealing with family issues. By being aware of your personal energies during a particular year, you can focus on those activities that are most appropriate given the nature of that period.

As you will discover, knowledge of the numbers can be of tremendous value, saving time and eliminating much of the guesswork and frustration that might arise when planning a trip without a roadmap. By using your unique set of numbers, you can effectively map out the entire course of your journey. Your Birth Date alone will reveal the important numbers and cycles at work in your life including:

The Life Path Number

The Life Path is the most important of the numbers derived from the date of birth. It reflects the broad characteristics and traits of the lessons, challenges, and opportunities you will encounter and is in a way the main roadmap for your journey. Familiarity with this number alone can be very helpful when making important decisions, especially with respect to career and general life direction. Your Life Path number will help clarify why certain choices are more suitable than others.

CHAPTER 1 • INTRODUCING THE NUMBERS

The Birth Day Number

The number of the day you were born describes specific attributes at your disposal and provides important indicators as to the type of career or occupation that would be most suitable for you.

The 9-Year Epicycle

This very important cycle, including the Personal Year, Personal Month, and Personal Day numbers, describes the short- to medium-term periods encountered along the way and gives you the clearest picture of where you have been, where you are, and where you are going. This book will focus mainly on this cycle, in particular, the Personal Year, as it provides the most comprehensive system of knowledge for planning.

The Pinnacles

These cycles describe trends, opportunities, areas of interest, and potential for important learning along the way. They give the overall tone of specific periods and, when combined with the Life Path and other numbers active at a given time, will help you address and deal with circumstances and also take full advantage of the opportunities at hand.

What Do These Numbers Mean?

I love numbers. For me, they convey knowledge, structure, order, and perhaps even the intelligence and the beauty of the movement of life. As a numerologist with decades of experience, it is understandable that the numbers speak to me perhaps in ways that others might not comprehend. For those with little or no experience with numerology, numbers can sometimes seem to carry mystical, even mysterious messages.

Now and then, someone asks for my take on a particular number, or group of numbers that keep showing up. It may be a pair of numbers such as the time on a clock, such as 11:11, or the numbers of a birthday, or a deceased family member's address. Some will use the numbers as a convenient scapegoat onto which they can project an inner fear or belief. For example, someone might say: "It's because of this recurring number 11 that I lost my way." Actually, if you lost your way, it's because you were not being mindful. The 11 was simply inviting you to pay attention. Whenever I see the number 11 I have to smile because it reminds me of an old television show from the 60s, "My Favourite Martian," in which the Martian, played by Ray Walston, had a pair of very primitive-looking antennas sticking off the top of his cap. For me, the antennas, or the 11, convey the idea of a deeper connection with the inner self and guidance when turned inward. When turned outward, the 11 can indicate confusion or distraction due to an overabundance of external noise. Balancing your focus between the inner and the outer is important.

Numerology can shed light on the most profound situations as well as the purely mundane. The information derived from the numbers depends on the breadth of perception of the interpreter, the frame of reference and life experience, as well as the ability to apply the information in the context at hand. As you will discover, the numbers provide valuable, sometimes essential, information that may facilitate and enhance our life experience. They simply reflect back to us in a unique manner the circumstances of a situation or question. They are a form of language that has the ability to convey information on a variety of levels.

The best way for a non-numerologist to derive meaning from numbers that seem to show up repeatedly is to simply acknowledge their presence, and then to invite their meaning in. A cursory search for the meaning of numbers can be fun, but it should not become an obsession. Keep in mind that the numbers do not *cause* anything. Ultimately, what is important is the meaning they have for *you*. If their occurrence in your life causes you to feel anxious, fearful, or distracted, then pay them no mind. There is no purpose in chasing after meanings that keep you from your peace and prevent you from being present in the moment.

CHAPTER 1 • INTRODUCING THE NUMBERS

If the meaning of a particular number has true importance for you, somehow that meaning will be conveyed. It may show up on the side of a bus, on a social media post, or in a comment casually made in conversation with a neighbour. Know that if you have asked for their meaning, and such meaning serves purpose, it will be revealed. The numbers are our friends, our travel companions on the journey of life. Let the numbers speak to you, and have fun with them.

How to Work With the Numbers

Each number carries a unique energy signature and is defined by a specific body of attributes. When a number is associated with a person's life journey, as is the case with the Life Path number, it tells a story about the nature of that journey. As you will soon learn, the number 5 speaks of change, adventure, and experimentation, whereas the number 4 indicates stability, order, and structure.

With a basic understanding of the numbers at work in your life, it is possible to make choices that are appropriate for your particular energy signature. For example, you would not expect someone with a strong number 5 pattern to be content sitting behind a desk in a routine nine-to-five job—in fact, they would most likely grow resentful of their limiting circumstances and probably quit. The number 4 person, on the other hand, normally happy with a structured and ordered lifestyle, would feel insecure if they happened to lose that same routine job and found themselves suddenly faced with material uncertainty and unexpected change. The 4 person needs order and routine, while the 5 person seeks change and freedom.

In the practice of numerology, numbers are always reduced to a single digit, so that you will work mostly with the numbers 1 through 9, referred to in this book as the Basic numbers. For a birthday on the eighteenth of December, the number 18 would be reduced by adding the 1 and the 8, for a result of 9. December, the twelfth month, would be represented by the number 3, the result of adding 1 and 2. In working with Birth Dates, it is important to perform the calculations in the order specified throughout the book, or else important information derived from certain special numbers could be lost. Always reduce the numbers for the day, month, and year before completing the sum.

There are two exceptions when applying the rule of reduction: the numbers 11 and 22 are never reduced. For a November birthday, the eleventh month, you would use the number 11. For a birthday on November 22, use 11 and 22, rather than 4 (2 + 2) and 2 (1 + 1). The numbers 11 and 22 are called Master numbers. They tend to vibrate at a higher frequency than their single digit counterparts, and may indicate a larger potential than the simple 2 and 4. About 25 percent of the charts in my files contain a number 11 among the core numbers (the main numbers from the Birth Date and the Birth Name) and 15 percent contain a 22. In this book, you will find references to the Master numbers written in the following manner: 11/2 and 22/4, and expressed as "eleven-two" and "twenty-two-four."

The High Energy numbers constitute another group of special numbers. The numbers 13, 14, 16, and 19 have traditionally been called the Karmic Debt numbers. However, I prefer to call them "High Energy" numbers as the term "karmic debt" can carry a negative tone, which is not at all required or even helpful. The High Energy numbers are like a red flag, pointing to potential challenges in manifesting their Basic number, or single-digit counterpart, in a positive way. They are generally written as 13/4, 14/5, 16/7, and 19/1. Although reduced to single digits in all calculations—13 reduces to 4 (1 + 3), 14 reduces to 5 (1 + 4), 16 reduces to 7 (1 + 6), and 19 reduces to 1 (1 + 9 = 10; 1 + 0 = 1)—these double-digit numbers are taken into consideration in the final analysis.

For example, a Life Path with a sum of 13 is reduced to 4, but the number 13 would be considered as being *behind* the number 4. The result can be expressed simply as "thirteen-four." The High

CHAPTER 1 · INTRODUCING THE NUMBERS

Energy numbers represent additional lessons that need to be learned before the energy of the Basic number can be expressed in a completely harmonious and productive manner. Over one-third of the charts in my files contain one High Energy number among the core numbers, one-quarter contain two, and fewer contain three or four.

The Language of Numbers

As you begin to work with the numbers, you will discover that they have a language of their own. Each number is like an archetype, manifesting an energy that expresses itself in a distinctive set of characteristics. These characteristics can vary from positive and constructive to negative or even destructive. Each person has a unique relationship (ranging from positive to negative) with each of the numbers, even with those numbers that do not figure prominently in their core numbers. In fact, the lack or absence of a number is a relationship of sorts, which, as we will soon see, is an important consideration. Take the time to become familiar with the traits of each number. This will make it easier for you to apply the knowledge of the numbers to your particular circumstances.

As you read the keywords in the following section, notice how the numbers are like a complete system, with attributes and traits evolving and flowing from one to the next, like a stream widening its flow as it merges with other streams, growing into a large river, ending its journey where it joins the sea. So too the human experience builds and grows more complex as we move from the singleness of the 1 to the tension and duality of the 2. The merging of two then explodes with creative force in the 3. In order to not be engulfed in a chaotic surge of creativity, the 3 adds a 1 for stability. So we find order and structure in the 4, only to be stimulated once again into movement and change by the addition of a 1 to the 4, for the destabilizing energy of the adventurous 5. The 6 represents even more complex energies at work, comprised of three pairs of 2s, or two pairs of 3s, generating a sense of responsibility toward others with a need for balance and harmony. The 7 adds an additional element of specialness with a lone 1 added to the responsible, balanced 6. The 8 manifests the ultimate worldly and material accomplishment with its pair of 4s and four 2s. The 9, the result of the addition of a 1 to the 8, brings us to a point of completion and wholeness, leading inevitably to a great release, in preparation for a new beginning. What was meant to be has become; what is yet to be has not yet been defined. And the cycle begins anew. This process of birth, growth and completion is reflected in the 9-Year Epicycle, and on a yearly basis in the Personal Month numbers.

The following list of keywords portrays the characteristics of each of the Basic numbers 1 through 9, as well as those of the Master numbers 11 and 22, and the High Energy numbers 13, 14, 16, and 19. Familiarize yourself with the basic traits of each number. Refer to this list after calculating your numbers in the chapters that follow. By using these keywords, it will be easy for you to obtain plausible interpretations for given periods of your life.

The goal of this work is to provide the tools that will facilitate improved self-understanding as well as stimulate your insights and creativity during the planning stages of your activities. Being in the right place at the right time means that you know yourself and also have a keen sense of timing, two essential ingredients for achieving personal success. A basic understanding of your numbers will give you that ability.

The Basic Numbers

Number 1

New beginnings, initiative, renewal, individuality, energy, rebirth, creativity, inventiveness, adventure, courage, assertiveness, will, determination, pride, leadership, entrepreneurship, inspiration, autonomy, self-reliance, independence, innovation, enterprise, opening up to new horizons, reorientation, focus on

CHAPTER 1 • INTRODUCING THE NUMBERS

self, drive, authority, executive ability, progressiveness, breaking from the past, establishing new patterns, creating new habits, setting new plans into motion.

When out of balance: selfishness, insensitivity, impulsiveness, having an overbearing personality, dictatorial behaviour, stubbornness, bossiness, self-centeredness, laziness, apathy, greed, narrow-mindedness, impatience, low self-esteem, shyness, retiring personality, self-deprecation, insecurity, cowardliness, helplessness, meekness, weak will.

Number 2

Relationships, cooperation, sensitivity, mediation, receptivity, reaction, conciliation, collaboration, consideration for others, teamwork, focus on the needs of others, partnership, reliance on the goodwill of others, service, flexibility, affection, sincerity, adaptability, attentiveness, kindness, romance, love, hospitality, graciousness, support, sympathy, tact, tolerance, devotion, loyalty.

When out of balance: dependency, indecision, shyness, neediness, oversensitivity, apathy, snobbery, rudeness, obstinacy, fear, taking things personally, insensitivity, rudeness, unclear boundaries with others, second-guessing oneself, co-dependency, lack of self-reliance, moodiness, negativity.

Number 3

Communications, creativity, optimism, heightened mental activity, sociability, fun, community involvement, inspiration, entertainment, enjoyment of life, having a good time, self-expression, drama, relaxation, artistic ability, the lighter side of life, luck, enthusiasm, affection, imagination, kindness, loquaciousness, charm and wit, originality, hospitality, style, image, humour, youthful spirit.

When out of balance: disorganization, chaos, superficiality, gossip, empty promises, wastefulness, indiscretion, childishness, tactlessness, unkindness, pettiness, envy, pessimism, procrastination, over-dramatization, vanity, inability to concentrate, lack of attention, meanness, unpleasantness, coarseness, criticism, negativity, depression, moodiness, immaturity.

Number 4

Focus, order, structure, foundations, organization, work, determination, fortitude, practicality, service, purpose, health, money, home, routine, family, fundamentals, honesty, loyalty, day-to-day matters, paying attention to details, matters requiring dedication, discipline, persistence and patience, trustworthiness, reliability, dependability, responsibility, management, rigorousness, thoroughness, traditional values, business, steadfastness, commitment.

When out of balance: getting stuck in a rut, inflexibility, need to control, perfectionism, negative attitude, feelings of limitation, fear, monotony, resentment, selfishness, meanness, resistance, envy, dogmatism, narrow-mindedness, laziness, impracticality, wastefulness, stubbornness, rudeness, callousness, obstinacy, lacking in purpose, focus and direction.

Number 5

Freedom, liberation, variety, release from the drudgery of day-to-day responsibilities, expansion, movement, growth, creativity, versatility, exploration of new horizons, lifting of restrictions, pushing away boundaries, travel, adventure, experimentation, new experiences, originality, progressiveness, creativity, inspiration, resourcefulness, multi-talented, sociability, change and unexpected events.

When out of balance: impatience, anger, frustration, choosing freedom over responsibility, inability to focus, erratic or inconsistent behaviour, seeking change for its own sake, instability, unreasonable risk taking, undependability, unreliability, lack of dedication and focus, failure to learn from experience, inflexibility, overindulgence in pleasurable activities.

CHAPTER 1 · INTRODUCING THE NUMBERS

Number 6

Responsibility, family, love, focusing on the needs of others, accountability to oneself and to others, healing, service, stability, understanding, devotion, justice, balance, creativity, artistic ability, seeking harmony in the environment and in relationships, protectiveness, romance, helpfulness, trustworthiness, dedication, generosity, peacefulness, being helpful to family members, coworkers and friends.

When out of balance: meddling, blurred boundaries with others, inability to say no, resentment of responsibilities, over involvement in the affairs of others, pride, worry, anxiety, jealousy, cynicism, small-mindedness, unkindness, pettiness, selfishness, meanness, insensitivity, vindictiveness, manipulation, smothering, possessiveness, insecurity, pessimism, hopeless victim or victimizer, negativity, excessive idealism.

Number 7

Analysis, introspection, reflection, thinking, isolation, time-out, meditation, need for solitude, understanding, deepening the learning experience, specialization, study, focus, clarity, silence, subtlety, being informed, creativity, need for space and privacy, spiritual quest, studiousness, analysis, profundity, looking beneath the surface of all things, seeking the meaning of life, reason and rationality, scientific mind, problem-solving ability.

When out of balance: pessimism, secrecy, confusion, criticism, feelings of superiority over others, plotting, suspicion, cheating, negativity, doubt, deceit, selfishness, antisocial behaviour, scepticism, fear, simple-mindedness, dullness, self-consciousness, childishness, insincerity, superficiality, thoughtlessness, imprudence, foolhardiness, dishonesty, narrow-mindedness, ignorance.

Number 8

Power, realization of goals, achievement, authority, the peak of accomplishment, maximum results, confidence, rewards, recognition, money, wealth, drive, ambition, success, management ability, organizational skills, leadership, boldness, responsibility, making things happen, realism, practicality, dependability, loyalty, strong personality, entrepreneurship, vision, efficiency, good judgment, directness, honesty, straightforwardness, focus and dedication.

When out of balance: insensitivity, dogmatism, greed, domineering or overbearing personality, intolerance, poor judgment, materialism, excessive ambition, demanding, unrealistic expectations, arrogance, selfishness, weak will, shyness, irresponsibility, stubbornness, acquisitiveness, procrastination, lack of focus, vision and direction.

Number 9

Humanitarian endeavours, philanthropy, the big picture, charity, selflessness, empathy, compassion, completion, endings, social consciousness, community-mindedness, inclusiveness, broad vision, imagination, creativity, the arts, sensitivity, perfectionism, releasing the past, preparing for the future, passion, drama, consideration, sympathy, inspiration, sociability, love, readiness to be of service, helpfulness, generosity, idealism, sense of fairness and justice.

When out of balance: selfishness, self-indulgence, resentment, criticism, negativity, lack of gratitude, drama, insensitivity, projection, blame, excessive idealism, emotionalism, aimlessness, drifting, fickleness, unrealistic expectations, discouragement, outrageous goals, inability to share emotions, unkindness, apathy, short-sightedness, lack of vision and imagination.

The Master Numbers

The Master numbers 11 and 22 are given special consideration, and are the only numbers not reduced to a single digit when calculating results. Their energy is often not manifested to its full positive potential until later in life, when a certain level of

CHAPTER 1 · INTRODUCING THE NUMBERS

self-awareness and maturity has been developed. Sometimes, the positive potential is never fully expressed. Individuals with a Master number in their core numbers often have a deep feeling of special purpose in life. It takes courage and positive support from family and the environment to manifest this potential.

Number 11

Like an intensified, or highly sensitive number 2, the 11 is the number of subtle relationships, sometimes acting as a link between this world and others beyond. People with 11s are usually highly intuitive. It confers sensitivity, idealism, progressiveness, imagination, vision, mysticism, uniqueness, a sense of special purpose or specialness, and tends to be emotional and often dramatic. It sometimes gives a heightened sixth sense that can be used in a helping profession. It's important to pay attention to where those antennas are turned: inward, or outward.

When out of balance: excessive sensitivity to people and to the environment, self-absorption, fanaticism, drama, irresponsibility, lack of realism and good judgment, impracticality, superiority complex, inflexibility, narrow-mindedness, difficulty finding a place in the world.

Number 22

Like a more expansive and ambitious number 4, the number 22 is the Master Builder, seeking great and tangible accomplishment. It gives big ideas, vision, a sense of personal power, and tends to be highly ambitious. Its energy is not easily harnessed in the early years of life, and even later, unless a conscious effort is made at bringing out its full potential, is not often fully developed. The 22 is inventive, inspiring, enterprising, strong, resourceful, generous, giving, productive, creative, progressive, and a leader and great problem solver.

When out of balance: scheming, feelings of inferiority, resentment of responsibilities, vengeful, lack of accomplishment, wasting of talents, a sense of worthlessness, frustration, anger, lack of direction and focus, inability to accomplish goals, selfishness, stubbornness, wastefulness.

The High Energy Numbers

The High Energy numbers 13, 14, 16, and 19 denote areas that require special attention, challenging situations, and personality traits that can only be corrected through conscious application and learning. Ignoring these traits will usually delay or hinder your progress. Until their lessons are learned and the energy is expressed effectively, these numbers tend to manifest in an imbalanced way.

Each High Energy number carries the traits of the single digit to which it is reduced, but these traits are usually expressed in an exaggerated or distorted manner. With self-awareness, conscious application, growth and learning, the weakened or distorted energy of a High Energy number can be transmuted into the positive expression and often into a far superior manifestation of its single digit counterpart. It is particularly important when found in the Life Path number.

If your birthday is the 13th, 14th, 16th, or 19th of any month, you have a High Energy number among your core numbers. High Energy numbers provide additional information about the challenges, but more importantly, the learning opportunities you may encounter.

Note that it is easy for beginner students of numerology to panic and become overly concerned when encountering a High Energy number at work in their cycles. As we have seen, High Energy numbers are quite common. Simply consider it as a more advanced lesson requiring additonal attention and effort, which can, once mastered, lead to superior results. I have five High Energy numbers among my core numbers. Sometimes those challenging numbers can serve to push us forward on our path!

CHAPTER 1 • INTRODUCING THE NUMBERS

Number 13/4

The lesson that needs to be learned with the 13 High Energy number is appreciation for hard work. The 13 can indicate selfishness (1) and a tendency for laziness and the avoidance of, or resentment toward the restrictions and limitations of life (3). Persons marked by the 13/4 tend toward negative, rigid and dogmatic thinking and can be heard whining and complaining about how difficult life is, or how they wish they could just quit their job, or whatever situation they feel is restrictive. They may have an underlying feeling that their life is unfairly difficult, that there are always obstacles to be overcome, and that they never seem to get a break. Luck is definitely not on their side. Developing an appreciation for and positive attitude for hard work, service, order, diligence and attention to detail, releases the tremendous power inherent in the 4, resulting in a potential for substantial material gain and personal accomplishment.

Number 14/5

The 14 High Energy number represents a lesson in moderation and balance. The individual struggles with a desire for freedom (1), and sometimes will seek it at any cost, even abandoning stability and security (4). The 14/5 often manifests as a tendency for impatience, for doing too much or taking on more than can reasonably be handled. Individuals marked by the 14/5 can be highly erratic, impulsive, and inconsistent, and tend to avoid commitment for fear of loss of personal freedom. They experience much change in their lives, and often leave a trail of incomplete life experiences. Failing to learn from these experiences, they repeat the same errors over and over again. They need to learn to be flexible and open to new opportunities while remaining focused on their goals. Through the conscious application of moderation and a willingness to make long-term commitments, the number 14/5 can be transformed to manifest tremendous creative versatility.

Number 16/7

The 16 High Energy number brings a lesson of depth and integrity of experience. This High Energy number marks the struggle between selfish desires (1) and the necessity for service and love of others (6). Individuals marked by the 16/7 are often isolated and introspective, withdrawing from the very interaction they need to heal their inherent selfishness. They avoid open interaction for fear of being criticized, hurt, or rejected. They may have difficulty finding satisfactory relationships. Overly analytical, they can be highly critical and judgemental, and can easily feel superior to others. Their tendency to seek answers deep within gives them the advantage of being able to learn some of the deeper lessons of life. Those with the 16/7 often undergo several major life-transforming experiences throughout their lives. By learning humility, adopting a positive attitude, and overcoming their relationship fears, 16/7 individuals can access their great potential for analysis through learning and expanding their understanding of the human condition.

Number 19/1

The 19 High Energy number represents a lesson in tolerance and balanced self-love. Individuals marked by the 19/1 can be overly wilful, stubborn, and too independent. In the 19, self-centered interests (1) are extended into all ambitions (9) or, on the opposite side, submerged by fear and lack of courage. The result is a potential for an attitude of intolerance and abuse of power toward others. If the individual has self-confidence issues, the 19 can manifest as an inability to act and pursue desires and ambitions. Individuals marked by the 19/1 may have a sense of entitlement and believe that the world revolves around them. They need to learn love, tolerance and acceptance of others. Once the negative aspects of the number have been consciously mastered and its lessons learned, it indicates tremendous potential for enviable success and happiness in all areas of life.

CHAPTER 1 • INTRODUCING THE NUMBERS

Planning for the Future

Time is perceived as being linear. Looking back, most people can trace the significant and not-so-significant events of their lives from early childhood to adulthood: the first day of school, a trip with the family, a move, family breakup, a first kiss, death of a grandparent, graduation day, a first job, marriage, birth of a child, divorce...

For as long as I can remember, the future has presented itself in my mind in a linear fashion too, like a timeline unfolding straight ahead, with markers for months, seasons, special events like holidays, business events, family gatherings, and year ends. There is bright sunshine and budding greenery for springtime; bold flowers and more sunshine for summer; the hues of deep orange, reds and yellows and darkening skies mark autumn; and cold gray and white for winter. (I guess you wouldn't be surprised if I told you I also dream in colour.)

However, I do take these images simply as symbols of the general trends ahead, acting as a backdrop for planning and setting goals for the future. I place only required and scheduled events on this timeline, leaving the details to unfold as they arise. Preferring to rely on inner guidance for most of my decisions, I've always shied away from setting too many specifics on my future timeline lest I prevent an important lesson or opportunity from presenting itself. Yet, the basic framework of a timeline frees me to plan more effectively, to schedule events and set goals for appropriate times, within realistic time frames, and to comfortably deal with situations and circumstances as they occur. This allows me to live mostly on a day-to-day basis without worrying about the future.

Wanting to make a point about planning for the future, I conducted a survey among family, friends, and clients. The question was as follows: when you look ahead into the future, how do events present themselves? I specified that I didn't want to know what their goals were, but rather how they saw their future unfolding. Did they see a road, a path, a calendar, or a line? To my great astonishment, I learned that although the past is generally perceived as being linear, very few people perceive their future in a linear fashion. Many see events in clumps around them, one week at a time, things that have to get done; others see the future as a sort of clock, or dial, with the future going around and sometimes spiralling upwards. One friend's future presents itself as a ladder, something she must climb. Only one person described her future as appearing on a line ahead of her.

A few people admitted to preferring not to look into the future for fear of what they might encounter, kind of like closing your eyes when you know that something bad is about to happen. They feel that they have enough to deal with in the present moment. Some who had experienced sales and motivational training were more apt to have specific goals, generally seen as hanging out there somewhere in the great beyond, commonly described as a big blue sky. However, given the absence of a timeline, they couldn't say exactly when they expected to reach these goals, or how they planned on reaching them. Others were content to not have specific goals and gave little thought to what might arise in the future. Yet all had wishes for the future: a happy retirement, good health, a nice big home, a special person to share the journey with, or the big career move they deeply desired. What they didn't have was the roadmap for getting there.

One of the powerful features of numerology is that it describes the cycles at work in our lives, cycles of varying length, from daily, monthly, and yearly to cycles that last many years. As you have seen, each number corresponds to a unique set of traits. The number 3 relates to communications, creativity, and social activity, while the number 4 reflects order, structure, and organization. When you incorporate your numerology cycles into your timeline for the future, the picture becomes even more interesting. For any given year there is a corresponding number that gives unique information about the trends for that year. This is called the Personal Year number. A person who engages in

CHAPTER 1 • INTRODUCING THE NUMBERS

activities that reflect the nature of this trend will be more likely to experience success than one who ignores it and chooses to engage in activities that are contrary to its nature.

Say that the number that corresponds to the current year is a 3. This means that my timeline for the year is coloured by the energy of the number 3. I would know that in order to take full advantage of the energies available to me at this time, I should focus my attention on developing my social network, tapping into my creativity, writing, and maybe even making a little time for fun and entertaining activities. The year that follows will have a number 4 energy, and should be a year of focus, structure, and organization, basically a work year. If I have taken time out to relax and enjoy myself in the 3 Personal Year, I will be refreshed and renewed, ready to buckle down to work in the 4 year. Also, any creative projects begun in the 3 year are likely to be structured and given greater form in the 4 year. Knowing my Personal Year cycles, I can focus on what needs to be done rather than worry about what I should do or whether or not I'm doing the right thing.

You may find this strange, but although I have practised astrology and numerology for nearly fifty years, I actually don't care to know my future, at least not in all its details. What would be the purpose of living if I knew everything in advance? Given my 14/5 Birth Day and Life Path numbers, I enjoy uncovering my potential and discovering opportunities for using my talents and abilities. Then why use numerology? There is a vast difference between knowing the details of your future and having a general sense of upcoming trends. One will take away your sense of discovery and adventure, while the other will strengthen your sense of purpose and direction. Imagine embarking on a voyage to a faraway destination without a roadmap. It would probably appear like a daunting, even impossible challenge. Knowledge of your numbers is similar to using a roadmap. The map remains your guideline; how you experience the journey is a combination of the choices you will make along the way, as well as factors beyond your control such as the weather, traffic, and events. Plus, says my 14/5, a good roadmap saves time!

Without limiting or confining you, your numbers will tell you the following:

- Where you are headed
- What type of experiences you are likely to encounter
- And how best to take advantage of your opportunities

Exercise: My Experience of the Numbers

As a first step in defining your life journey, it is essential that you have intimate knowledge of the one making the journey—*you*. Self-knowledge is an essential ingredient to successful planning and decision making. You may already be familiar with your personality profile through consultation with a professional astrologer or numerologist or other tools such as Myers Briggs profiles. For those who are seeking to deepen their self-understanding, the following exercise has been included to help set the stage for the planning exercises in later chapters. Keep in mind that the better you know yourself, the more likely you are to make choices that best suit your unique needs, desires, values, talents, and abilities.

If, for example, you were about to encounter a period where the number 3 was highly active, and you were aware that you were lacking in the positive attributes of this number, such as communication and social skills, creativity, and a positive attitude, you could spend more time integrating its qualities into your life. The 3 period would then be much more rewarding and enriching.

We all, over time, slide from one end of the scale to the other, sometimes expressing the more positive attributes, at other times, the less favourable characteristics of a number's energy. As we grow in self-awareness and take responsibility for our decisions, responses and actions, we slide to the positive side. To manifest

CHAPTER 1 • INTRODUCING THE NUMBERS

the less positive qualities of a number, one only has to exaggerate or distort one of its basic traits. During periods of excessive stress, we can slide toward the less desirable expression of our numbers. Overall, the average person will express mostly the positive traits most of the time.

Also keep in mind that not all of the positive attributes of a number can be expressed fully at first try. Because a person has an 8 Life Path, it does not necessarily follow that they will automatically be comfortable and effective in a function as leader and director. A certain amount of experience and maturity is required in order to fully manifest the positive traits of this number. Nor will a person with a 6 Life Path automatically find perfect love just because it is in the nature of the number to seek and attract harmonious and loving relationships. I know of many 6 Life Path individuals who have enjoyed long stretches of single life, while there are many 5 Life Path individuals, a number usually associated with change and a strong need for freedom, who are happily married for the duration of their lives to the same partner. There are therefore a variety of possible expressions for each number, and what we make of our numbers is very much up to our choice.

The important thing is to be sufficiently aware of your experience of each of the numbers so that when one is activated in your life, you will better know how to respond. If you recognize that you have an excess of the number 1 energy, a 2 Personal Year might prove to be particularly challenging in the area of your personal relationships since it requires that you be flexible, receptive, and aware of the needs of others. On the other hand, this same overabundance of number 1 energy can become superexcited and exaggerated in a 1 Personal Year, causing you to be more independent and creative, but also perhaps more aggressive or wilful than normal.

Another point to keep in mind is that you may experience the numbers differently at various times of your life. The serious and private temperament of the 7 will serve someone well in a career that requires research and analysis without causing too many problems of solitude, whereas that same 7 might have been a difficult energy to deal with if, as a child, the person was surrounded by outgoing personality types.

In the following paragraphs, pay special attention to the descriptions that push your buttons. Okay, some of the character traits aren't very flattering, but everyone has their dark side. While we may occasionally swing away from the ideal, like the pendulum, we always return to the middle, in search of balance. Note that each person experiences the full range of energies manifested by the numbers. You may find that you resonate with two or three in particular. You may also resonate more with certain numbers at different periods of your life. When you apply the numerological cycles to your personal timeline, you may be startled by the relevance of your observations.

After reading the descriptions of each number, rate yourself as being deficient, balanced, or overabundant. While balanced sounds nice, being aware of an imbalance will help you be more effective in addressing what needs to be healed and tended to. Be honest with yourself—nobody's watching. Be matter-of-fact and curious, rather than critical, and have fun with it.

My Experience of the Number 1

Balanced Expression of 1 Energy

If your relationship with the energy of the number 1 is well balanced, then you enjoy a healthy dose of self-reliance, autonomy, and independence. You like to direct the flow of your life on your own terms. You are original, creative, intuitive, and generally active, and have excellent leadership, executive, and administrative potential. You like to start projects and then move on to something new. Your energy and drive inspire others to higher levels of performance.

Deficient or Underexpressed 1 Energy

A lack of 1s may manifest as a lack of assertiveness and even laziness. You lack motivation and rely on others to get things done. You avoid doing many of the things you dream of doing because they just seem like too much work. Sometimes you will give in to the demands of others because you are afraid to stand up for yourself. You lack firmness and assertiveness, and have little faith in your judgment or in your abilities.

Overabundance of 1 Energy

You tend to be dominant and overly aggressive, and will do almost anything to get your way. The world centers on you; you like to be centre stage. Your selfishness will cause rifts in your relationships as you trample over the feelings of others. You are wilful, stubborn, bossy, and egotistical.

My Experience of the Number 2

Balanced Expression of 2 Energy

The balanced 2 energy manifests as an awareness of the concerns of others and an ability, and probably a preference for, working with others in a group situation or partnership. Your main qualities include tact, adaptability, cooperation, modesty, receptivity, diplomacy, and sensitivity to the needs of others. You can handle delicate situations with grace, equanimity, and distinction. You have excellent social and people skills, yet are modest and can be a bit shy. You are an attentive, supportive, and affectionate lover and seek harmony in your relationships.

Deficient or Underexpressed 2 Energy

You come on like a bull in a china shop, insensitive to the needs of others. You lack tact, diplomacy, and sensitivity and can say things that are injurious to others without being aware of it. You prefer to do things by yourself, even going out of your way to avoid asking for help. You resent those circumstances when you must work as a team. You get impatient, especially when it is necessary to wait for someone else before you can do what you want to do.

Overabundance of 2 Energy

You are overly sensitive to the needs and opinions of others, sometimes going overboard in your eagerness to please and find love. You then feel resentment when people do not reciprocate with gratitude and service. You can be shy and fearful. In fact, your definition of who you are is based on what others say about you. You tend to take things too personally. Your need for love, affection, and attention seems to be insatiable, causing problems in your personal relationships. You seek the ideal relationship, a fantasy that lies only in your mind.

My Experience of the Number 3

Balanced Expression of 3 Energy

When well balanced, the number 3 shows a generous talent for self-expression. Often the 3 energy manifests in an artistic field. You enjoy sharing ideas and fun times with others. You are considered to be the entertainer of your group, the life of the party, always one to enjoy a good laugh and to have a good time. Your artistic and creative talents may remain dormant. You are sociable, witty, happy-go-lucky, joyful, gracious, and charming. People easily gravitate toward you.

Deficient or Underexpressed 3 Energy

You are very self-critical, stopping yourself from ever expressing your inner inspiration. You suffer from acute "perfectionitis", so you will find something wrong with your performance no matter what. Overly serious and fearful of criticism, often with a pessimistic outlook, it is difficult for you to simply enjoy yourself and appreciate what you have.

Overabundance of 3 Energy

You tend to take things much too lightly, adopting a cavalier attitude, especially when the finger gets pointed in your direction. You are disorganized, trite, and superficial, and spend far too much time gossiping. You are wasteful and scatter your energy in questionable activities. Having difficulty seeing into the depth of situations, you can miss the point.

My Experience of the Number 4

Balanced Expression of 4 Energy

You are conscientious, an excellent organizer and very hard working. You are the quintessential worker bee, appreciating order, routine, and stability in all things. You are practical, conservative, patient, down-to-earth, and approach new circumstances with caution and reason. You are an excellent planner and can tend to the many details and intricacies of a project. You are responsible, loyal, honest, and reliable. Family, home and financial security are important to your well-being.

Deficient or Underexpressed 4 Energy

You may have difficulty finding your place in the material world. You function more with intuition than with order, method, and discipline. Your ideals are lofty; you are a free spirit and prefer to not have to deal with the drudgery and details of day-to-day routine. You are impractical and disorganized, dislike limitations of all kinds, and find it difficult, even impossible, to follow a daily work routine. Even if you appreciate order, somehow you just can't get yourself organized.

Overabundance of 4 Energy

You are overly rigid in your thinking, and can be bossy, stubborn, and dogmatic. You are too much of a disciplinarian, behaving at times like a battlefield general rather than an understanding superior. You easily become submerged in details, losing track of the big picture. You give the impression of being stodgy, stern, controlling, dull, and stuck in a rut. You may be motivated by deep-seated fear.

My Experience of the Number 5

Balanced Expression of 5 Energy

Healthy 5 energy manifests as a progressive attitude and outlook. You are often ahead of the times in your field of expertise, and are usually adventurous, creative, multitalented, and versatile. You are an excellent communicator and sales person, and have original ways of presenting your ideas. You enjoy working with people, have an entertaining and often fascinating personality, and are clever, witty, and analytical. You enjoy change and exploring new possibilities. Freedom is a key ingredient of your happiness.

Deficient or Underexpressed 5 Energy

You dislike change and are closed to new ideas, easily threatened by anything that might upset the status quo. You don't adapt well to new circumstances. You lack vision and imagination and don't function well outside of your routine. You prefer to cling to the old familiar ways of doing things. You fear life, adventure, risk, and new experiences.

Overabundance of 5 Energy

You are restless, inconsistent, and impatient, lacking in sustained effort, tending to quit situations and relationships before they reach completion. It is difficult for you to maintain a routine, and you may lack the discipline and perseverance required to reach your goals. Any new thing that comes along can throw you off course and cause you to lose focus. You can overindulge in sensual pleasures, or in any activity you enjoy. You fail to learn from experience because you move on too quickly.

My Experience of the Number 6

Balanced Expression of 6 Energy

You have a caring, friendly, sympathetic disposition, and enjoy helping others. You are conscientious and responsible, the one others turn to for help. Always ready to contribute to the betterment of the community, it is not uncommon to find yourself involved in some type of volunteer capacity. You have a strong sense of justice, artistic sensitivity, and may express healing ability. You are the ideal employee, an outstanding manager, and find fulfillment in a position of service. In all things, you seek stability, balance, and harmony.

Deficient or Underexpressed 6 Energy

Due to your difficulty in forming harmonious relationships with others, you struggle with solitude and unsatisfying relationships. Preferring to do things on your own, you try to avoid responsibilities and are fearful of making commitments to others. "Till death do us part" frightens you. It is difficult for you to express your true feelings, and so you remain guarded, preventing the development of trust required to sustain long-term relationships.

Overabundance of 6 Energy

You tend to be overly concerned with the welfare of others, fussing and worrying, even meddling and interfering in the affairs of others, extending yourself well beyond your personal boundaries. You can grow resentful of your responsibilities and obligations. You are jealous, possessive, suspicious, and demanding in love. You are overly idealistic, seeking perfection in yourself and in others. It is difficult for you to find balance.

My Experience of the Number 7

Balanced Expression of 7 Energy

You have a strong mind, and tend to be deep, penetrating, analytical, and profound. You may also be very intuitive, although this attribute may not always be developed. You are inquisitive, intrigued by mystery and a lover of knowledge. You may have an interest in spirituality, philosophy, and the great unknown. You seem to be in some ways different from others, often marching to the beat of your own drum. You appreciate quiet and your time alone.

Deficient or Underexpressed 7 Energy

You prefer to remain on the surface of things, uninterested in digging for the deeper meaning of life. This prevents you from developing your full potential in many areas. You are not interested in the true meaning of situations. Ill-informed, you tend to make inaccurate judgments and conclusions. You can be a slow learner.

Overabundance of 7 Energy

Overly involved with your own ideas and inner life, you show a lack of emotion, even coldness and superiority toward others. You can be overly analytical, suspicious, and tend to be highly critical and even intolerant of others. You can be a snob, and prefer your solitude to the company of others. Alienating others, you grow bitter and resentful of their lack of understanding of you.

My Experience of the Number 8

Balanced Expression of 8 Energy

You are a strong and powerful force in your environment, commanding respect, allegiance, and obedience. Energetic, self-confident, and a good judge of character, you are well suited for the corporate world. You have clear ambitions, and the drive, motivation, and organizational ability to reach your goals. You are practical, realistic, and dependable and can handle complex projects or situations.

Deficient or Underexpressed 8 Energy

You lack good judgment when it comes to money and possessions, causing you to experience fluctuations and material instability throughout your life. You fear your own power, and have difficulty with authority figures. Stubborn and impractical, you are resentful of being told what to do, yet powerless to reach your goals. You tend to be unrealistic, undisciplined, and lacking ambition and drive.

Overabundance of 8 Energy

You are overly rigid, stubborn, selfish, combative, despotic, and materialistic. Your excessive ambition makes you insensitive to the needs of others. Money, status, and power are very important to you, and you will seek these at any cost. You have a sense of entitlement, and can abuse the power invested in you, no matter how little it is.

My Experience of the Number 9

Balanced Expression of 9 Energy

You have universal appeal, and are someone that everyone likes. You are broad-minded, kind, fair, sympathetic, and agreeable. You are imaginative and creative, and can be a bit overly idealistic.

You can be a perfectionist, with yourself and with others. You enjoy participating in group or community projects, especially in anything that contributes to the well-being of the community at large. You don't mind setting your own interests aside for the welfare of others.

Deficient or Underexpressed 9 Energy

You lack sensitivity, compassion and understanding, and don't deal well with emotions, either your own, or other people's. You can be indifferent, uncooperative, and uncaring. You tend to be self-centered, unkind, unforgiving, and intolerant. It is difficult for you to set your own ambitions and needs aside for those of others. You have a narrow, rigid outlook on life and don't adapt well to new ideas.

Overabundance of 9 Energy

You tend to be a daydreamer and can be naïve, impractical, unrealistic, and overly emotional—a "diva" of sorts, expecting to have your every little whim catered to. You can be inconsistent, petty, changeful, unreliable, and uncooperative. You may blame others and the world for your situation, while it is your own unwillingness to assume responsibility for yourself that is the cause of your problems.

CHAPTER 2

Your Personal Life Roadmap

The Life Path Number

Among the numbers derived from your Birth Date, the Life Path number is by far the most important as it describes the terrain of your life's journey. Knowledge of this number, how it manifests in your life, and how you make use of its qualities and attributes is an essential component to determining your success. Some roads are hilly, others have sharp curves and bends, and others are relatively flat. Some trace the rugged coastline, others climb high into the mountains, while others cut through golden prairies.

Depending on the nature of the road you must travel, you will modify your approach to your journey. Each person's path is unique and should be approached in accordance with needs, age, and experience. What is easy for one may be challenging for another. Then again, what may have been challenging at one point in your life may have become easy with age, maturity, and experience. Hence the benefits of periodically standing back and doing an exercise such as "Where Am I Now?" at the end of this chapter.

Your Life Path number essentially describes the nature of the opportunities as well as the lessons and challenges you are likely to encounter along the way. Difficult stretches of road may require careful attention, but at the same time can motivate you to be more resourceful and creative, pushing you to make greater use of your talents and abilities. Smooth, straight roads are easy to navigate, but can also become boring and lacking in personal rewards as they are less challenging, requiring less use of talents and abilities. In working with clients, I have observed that overly easy periods can bring about less progress and fewer accomplishments than challenging ones, which require that you dig deep and work much harder. On the other hand, when used productively, smooth, easy stretches can be very helpful in giving you the opportunity to rest, stand back, and regroup. Taking a breather now and then can be very worthwhile.

Understanding the nature of your Life Path, with its periodic twists and turns, will enable you to not only have a clearer picture of your destination, but also to plot a more effective course toward your intended goals.

Calculation Methods

There are various methods for working with the numbers. However, as illustrated in the following example, they do not necessarily produce the same results. In this book, Method 1 is used, where each number is reduced to a single digit, with the exception of the Master numbers 11 and 22. You will notice that in the methods illustrated, while the final result is the same, the number *before* the final result is different. This number can provide additional information, especially if it is a High Energy number. Example calculations for August 14, 1954:

	Method 1	Method 2
	8	8
	5	14
	<u>1</u>	<u>1954</u>
	14	1976
	14/5	**23/5**

Method 3 $8 + 1 + 4 + 1 + 9 + 5 + 4 = 32$ **32/5**

CHAPTER 2 • YOUR PERSONAL LIFE ROADMAP

Calculating the Life Path Number

The Life Path number is easy to calculate. First reduce the numbers of your Month, Day, and Year of birth to single digits. Then add these numbers, and again reduce to a single digit, as needed. As mentioned in Chapter 1, the numbers 11 and 22 are not reduced. For example, for a person whose Birth Date is March 29, 1982, you would proceed as follows:

Birth Month	3	3	3
Birth Day	29	2+9	11
Birth Year*	1982	20	2
			16/7

*1982 is reduced as follows: 1 + 9 + 8 + 2 = 20, reduces to 2.

Add the reduced numbers from the Month, Day, and Year of birth: 3 + 11 + 2 = 16. Reduce to a single digit: 1 + 6 = 7. Note if there is a High Energy number behind the Life Path, a 16 *behind* the 7, for example. This will have a bearing on how the energies of the Life Path are likely to be manifested. A certain amount of conscious effort may be required before the full positive range and potential of the Life Path can be expressed.

The 1 Life Path

This is the Life Path of the individualist. You are driven by pure energy, which is often manifested in leadership skills and entrepreneurial spirit, as well as a great need for independence. You are self-motivated, autonomous, pioneering, resourceful, imaginative, inventive, creative, and goal-oriented. Before you can fully manifest your potential, you may need to develop confidence in your abilities and tap into the natural self-reliance that is part of your nature. Experience and maturity will bring you what you need to be successful.

Individuals with the 1 Life Path are ready and prepared to focus on their goals and ambitions. You prefer to make your own way in life with as little support from others as possible. Your independent nature can prove to be a blessing, as it enables you to forge ahead, but at times it can be a curse, as you can disregard the needs of others while seeking to reach your own goals. Your journey often involves the breaking of new ground in your field of interest. You do not easily seek out the help of mentors, preferring to make it on your own. You may be concerned with how you appear to others, wanting to give a good impression, one that smacks of success. Your pride can hold you back; you need to be reminded that sometimes it's okay to ask for help.

You can at times forget to look beyond your own boundaries and may even become uncaring or selfish. The conscious development of an awareness of the world outside yourself can be very beneficial. Your interests are varied, and your potential for success is enormous. Occupational fields include business, management, the arts, and community affairs, all areas in which you can be creative and express a leadership role.

If you have a High Energy 19 behind your number 1 Life Path, you may struggle with large-scale dreams and a desire to satisfy your own personal desires. You need to find a balance between tending to your needs and being sensitive and aware of the needs of others. You should guard against a tendency to be overly aggressive, trampling over others to reach your goals. There may be times when you feel alone and unsupported, but then again, you are often too proud and stubborn to ask for help. There is tremendous potential for creative leadership and personal success with this Life Path number, once its lessons have been learned.

If you have a 1 Life Path child, consider encouraging his or her self-reliance and independence. A healthy sense of self-awareness should be cultivated rather than inhibited, otherwise, feelings of resentment and frustration could emerge in misguided outbursts, or even an outright battle against authority. At the same time, 1 Life Path children are naturally inclined to focus on themselves and need to be taught to be considerate and compassionate toward others.

The 2 Life Path

You are very sensitive to the needs of others, conciliatory in style, and an excellent companion, listener, mediator, and moderator. You long to be in the ideal relationship and prefer to do things in the company of others. You may not do as well in a solo enterprise as would a 1 or 5 Life Path unless it is a service-based business, in which case, you are likely to excel. Sometimes you tend to set your own needs aside in favour of the needs of others. This can lead you to make questionable choices of partnerships and relationships. You can be somewhat shy and sensitive and generally do not seek the limelight for yourself, preferring the anonymity of a behind-the-scenes role. You are highly perceptive, patient, diplomatic, and cooperative and can be quite content helping your partner attain success.

You have a genuine concern for the welfare of others, and are often the first to step up to help a friend in need. You are dependable, responsible, reliable, caring, thoughtful, loyal, and devoted. You are also adaptable and flexible. You prefer the comfort of quiet, peaceful environments. Individuals with the 2 Life Path make excellent therapists, peacemakers, teachers, counsellors, trainers, support staff, aids, coaches, partners, mentors, mediators, and healers. They make great administrative assistants.

Children with the 2 Life Path are very sensitive to the comments and even the mere facial or bodily expressions of their caregivers. They can take things far too personally and they need to be taught early in life that everything isn't always about them. They can be shy and will keep things inside for fear of what others might say or think. They are affectionate and eager to please others and will thrive in a peaceful, loving, and harmonious environment. They prefer the company of others to solitude.

The 3 Life Path

You have excellent communication skills, a lively and positive outlook, resilience, lots of charm, wit, and enormous creative potential. Individuals with the 3 Life Path are artists by nature and often excel in some form of creative self-expression. Sometimes these talents remain dormant, or are consciously set aside for many years and can, in a later, more quiet time of life, flourish into a very enriching and rewarding hobby or even a second career. Success in the arts requires discipline and dedication, attributes that don't come naturally to many 3s, and will need to be developed. You are a born entertainer, and are very often the life of the party.

You have more than your share of grace, style, and social skills. You are optimistic, a great motivator, easy-going, and like to enjoy life. You are naturally emotional and volatile, and can express your thoughts freely. Be aware of a tendency to be gossipy and superficial. You prefer to talk about a subject superficially rather than researching it thoroughly. Managing your own finances can be a challenge. You can be vulnerable, dramatic, and sensitive to criticism, and at times can be your own worst critic. You can be easily distracted and may lose track of your long-term goals. A hands-on, short-term approach may be helpful if you are having difficulty sticking to your plans. 3s can do well in sales, and all the arts, media, communications, and entertainment fields.

Children with the 3 Life Path are sociable and enjoy the company of others. They enjoy fun and play, and can find it difficult to focus on homework and other limiting activities. They are affectionate and tend to express themselves freely. However, they can say things off the top of their heads, sometimes not mindful of how their words might affect others. They might benefit from being taught to think before speaking, and also to allow others to share their thoughts. They also need to learn to be responsible and organized.

CHAPTER 2 • YOUR PERSONAL LIFE ROADMAP

The 4 Life Path

You are no doubt very well organized, hard working, grounded, and you may even welcome, even expect, structure and order in all things. Areas of life that are important to you include family, home, financial and material security, and stability. This is usually not the path of the risk taker. You do well in a structured environment, with a regular schedule, and can thrive in the routine of a nine-to-five workday. You must guard against becoming overly rigid and closed-minded in your habits, opinions and attitudes. 4s do enjoy their routines!

You may be fearful of change, hesitant to venture out into the world, limiting your experiences to familiar environments, even becoming a homebody. You don't mind working at home, even out of your basement. You flourish in jobs that require attention to detail and service. Individuals with the 4 Life Path can be found in banking, finance, business, construction, and all activities requiring organization and order. You are loyal, dedicated, trustworthy, reliable, honest, and not afraid of hard work. 4s are the workhorses of any enterprise or organization.

When there is a 13/4 High Energy behind your Life Path, your life journey may seem unusually fraught with obstacles, challenges, and limitations. You may lack self-confidence and can be profoundly fearful. You struggle under the heavy mantle of hard work. If you would simply buckle down and focus on the tasks at hand, you would find great rewards in your eventual accomplishments. You can be overly rigid in your attitudes and habits. Opinionated and closed-minded, you may miss opportunities by clutching to old patterns and behaviours. By developing self-confidence and a positive and open-minded attitude, you can be among the hardest working and most productive of all.

Children with the 4 Life Path are focused and hard working by nature. They need a secure and orderly home to feel safe and respond well to stability and routine. They can be taught the value of dedication, practice, and regularity. They do well in a structured and disciplined environment. But all work and no play can make junior a bit stiff, so he must also be taught that it's okay to schedule time for fun and games.

The 5 Life Path

You enjoy change, variety, and movement. You usually don't do well in office jobs. The nine-to-five cubicle is not the place for you! Although day-to-day routine is not your forte, you can work twice as long and twice as hard as anybody in an activity for which you feel a passion. You need to move about, always seeking excitement, new challenges, and stimulus. You must guard against changing for the sake of change alone. Prone to risk-taking, you tend to jump into new ventures without adequate forethought.

Freedom is key to this Life Path. You may feel resentful and become uncooperative if you find yourself trapped in an overly restrictive environment. You need to learn that in order to achieve anything of significance, you must develop constancy, dedication, and diligence. You are multitalented and can do many things well. You gravitate toward adventure, innovation, experimentation, careers involving communications, research and development, teaching, and entertainment, and given your need for freedom, you can do well as a self-employed worker and sales rep, provided you acquire enough discipline and order to work efficiently. You are flexible, original, very resourceful, adaptable, and creative. You like to live well and large, enjoying all the pleasures that life has to offer. Beware of a tendency to overindulge in those activities that bring you joy. You can be disorganized and lacking in focus.

If there is a High Energy 14 behind your 5 Life Path, this can indicate a more erratic and irregular journey. You lack forethought and can make impulsive decisions, which lead to error. You have difficulty completing what you start, being easily lead to newer, more exciting opportunities, and can fail to learn from experience. You fear limitation and avoid making long-term commitments, preferring personal freedom to devotion

CHAPTER 2 • YOUR PERSONAL LIFE ROADMAP

and dedication to service or job. You need to learn the benefits of sustained and committed efforts; otherwise, you will repeatedly fall short of your goals. Once your lessons are learned, you can successfully express your tremendous versatility, broad range of talents and abilities, innovation, and creativity in your career.

Children with the 5 Life Path need to be given opportunities to experiment and explore a variety of avenues throughout childhood. They are inquisitive, adventurous, and innovative. Strong individualists, they prefer to do things at their own pace and in their own way, and should not be held to the same standards of measure as their siblings or peers. Although quick learners, they may at times lose focus due to a tendency to seek freedom or excitement outside the daily routine of home and school. They have a very low threshold for boredom, and don't do well in overly rigid environments. They need to be taught the benefits of order and structure.

The 6 Life Path

Loving, caring, and kind, you naturally enjoy responsibility. You are socially involved, eager to be of help, and genuinely concerned with the welfare of others. The 6s are the nurturers, supporters, and caregivers of the world. You feel validated when in a position of service and helpfulness to others, and in fact need to be needed. You can easily become indispensable in your job or home environment. However, in your desire to be helpful, you can over-extend your boundaries and interfere in the affairs of others, becoming more meddlesome than helpful. Many 6s should learn discernment in their eagerness to help and to please others, otherwise they can become resentful of their extensive responsibilities. Know that it is not necessary to save the world in order to be loved.

You have excellent executive abilities as well as a fair dose of artistic sensitivity and creativity. You are charming, gentle, affectionate, and friendly. Individuals with the 6 Life Path make excellent managers. You are an able problem solver—fair, just, and reliable. Areas of interest include management, sales, service-based industries, the health fields and the healing arts, social work, teaching, the arts, human resources, consulting, customer service, entertainment, and hospitality.

Children with the 6 Life Path are affectionate and want to please parents and teachers. They can be the teacher's pets, and everyone's friends. They make friends easily, and can at times compromise their own judgment for the sake of having a place among friends. Stronger personality types can influence them. They need to be taught to stick to their own values, even at the risk of losing a friend along the way. The 6 Life Path often has creative and artistic abilities.

The 7 Life Path

This is the Life Path of the analyst, the philosopher, and the thinker. You are generally quiet, low key, somewhat secretive, and sometimes shy, at least in your younger years. You may choose to avoid drawing attention to yourself, preferring the safety of your spot in the corner, and can appear distant and aloof. Your challenge in life is to maintain your personal life private, while dealing with the affairs of the outside world. You can be quite comfortable working alone, preferring isolated, quiet environments. In fact, for the sake of your well-being, you need some alone time. Your tendency to withdraw into seclusion when you have personal issues can alienate others. You may be cold and rational in personal relationships, preferring not to express your feelings.

You must learn to be comfortable in your solitude, without feeling lonely. For that, a healthy dose of self-love and self-respect is required. You can become critical of others, even to the point of feeling superior. A positive attitude should be cultivated and maintained at all times. Often, feelings of specialness or of being different are experienced with this Life Path. You are a seeker of truth, knowledge, and understanding. You enjoy uncovering mysteries and thrive when intellectually challenged.

You can do well as a researcher, writer, teacher, expert, consultant, scholar, healer, therapist, analyst, priest, counsellor, problem solver, or investigator.

If you have a 16/7 High Energy Life Path number, you no doubt have additional lessons to learn. Subject to intense introspection and analysis, you may experience one or more important transformations in your life, akin to the phoenix rising from its ashes. Often, this lesson involves a reversal of financial fortune, or the experience of a Dark Night of the Soul. It is important that you look beyond the superficial and material and focus on integrating the deeper meaning of things. You may suffer intense shyness and self-consciousness. You must guard against a tendency toward cynicism, jealousy, mistrust, self-centeredness, excessive pride and feelings of specialness and superiority. Trust and faith are among your most important lessons. By developing trust in others, by being kind-hearted and compassionate, you will experience a deeply rewarding life.

Children with the 7 Life Path enjoy their time alone, playing quietly with their toys, enjoying time away from the hustle and bustle of school and organized social events. They need intellectual challenges and puzzles to thrive. They have many questions, but may keep them to themselves, not wanting to draw undue attention. They must learn to open up in a safe environment, with someone who will not criticize or analyze them. Being overly analytical, a positive and supportive environment is especially important during the early years.

The 8 Life Path

You have plenty of natural leadership abilities, charm, energy, and drive. You have definite ambitions for personal success and wealth; you work well with a plan and have specific goals and objectives to meet. You are practical, hands-on and down-to-earth. 8 is the number of power and worldly success. You will probably not be content until you have achieved something of importance. Individuals with the 8 Life Path tend to think big, talk big, act big, and like to look successful. Many 8s are actually the movers and the shakers of the world, the ones that make things happen.

You can be overbearing once you set out to reach your goals, sometimes trampling over anything and anyone that might stand in your way. You can be the proverbial bull in a china shop. You can be too busy with the big picture to see the small things in front of you. You must learn to consider the welfare of others as well as your own interests in all your undertakings. If you are an insecure 8, you can become frustrated at your inherent lack of power, taking power wherever you can find it, usually over those who are weaker than you. An 8 without a good working plan is likely to be frustrated and unhappy. They need to see results, the bottom line. A healthy 8 Life Path expresses itself as inspiration, leadership, motivation, and focused drive and ambition. It is the path of the entrepreneur, leader, manager, CEO, or director.

Children with the 8 Life Path want to go to the head of the class before they can walk! They do well if given tasks that will make them feel important and responsible. They don't do well standing at the back of the class waiting for their turn while the others get their chance to show their talents. They need to learn empathy and compassion, two traits that will serve them well over time. They understand the concept of responsibility very early on and can thrive on having important tasks assigned to them.

The 9 Life Path

You are a humanitarian at heart, a visionary, and you are sensitive and socially conscious. You have a deep-seated desire to do something to make the world a better place. You are idealistic, creative, kind-hearted, artistic, and imaginative. If you don't have a function in the world or the community, you will look for ways of expressing your generous nature by helping those who are close at hand. In a world of overwhelming materialism, this is not always an easy Life Path to fulfill. You are open to lending an ear; you are a great problem solver and can express compassion and understanding. You have a genuine concern for the welfare of others and can see the big picture in all things. Your idealism can lead you to be disappointed with the mediocre ways of the world.

Individuals with the 9 Life Path generally enjoy travel, and many will travel far and wide for their work or for pleasure. You can become discouraged by the harshness of events in the world and can be profoundly disturbed by images of war, hunger, violence, cruelty, or sickness. At times, your broad outlook can make you feel superior to others. You need to understand that your happiness depends on your ability to be selfless and to think of the greater good. Selfishness in the 9 leads to profound frustration, resentment, and unhappiness. Selflessness leads to feelings of joy and fulfillment.

Children with the 9 Life Path are sensitive to the needs and expressions of the people around them. They have refined minds and can thrive in a broad, renaissance-style education. They are idealistic, easily connect with nature and the arts, and can be perfectionists at work and play. They need to learn to accept things as they are, imperfect as they are. They also need to understand that they cannot change the world in an instant.

The 11/2 Life Path

You have many of the attributes of the 2 Life Path, but are much more emotionally charged and sensitive, as though plugged into a higher energy source. This intense energy can manifest physically, creating tension and sensitivity to the environment, but it is mostly felt mentally and emotionally. You may be inspired by inner guidance, or a higher source, and can in turn inspire others. Highly emotional and intuitive, you may find it difficult to be moderate or to adopt a middle ground in anything that you do. You are very idealistic, and sometimes impractical or unrealistic in the goals you set for yourself. You may perceive yourself as having a special purpose in life, sensing that you are different from others, with a unique mission to accomplish.

You must guard against developing an overly inflated sense of self-importance and specialness.

Individuals with the 11 Life Path often have difficulty staying connected to reality. You need to develop sufficient confidence and inner strength to feel comfortable with your life purpose. You will do better with a few years of experience under your belt. When expressed in a balanced manner, 11s can be profoundly inspired to contribute in an important way to the betterment of a unique aspect of the human experience. (Read also the description of the 2 Life Path.)

The 22/4 Life Path

You are the Master Builder, and since a young age you may have sensed a burning desire to accomplish something of great value and importance. You want to change the world, and in some way, make a difference. Your opportunities may appear limited in comparison to your desire for accomplishment, and you may have difficulty finding your place in the world. You have great management, organizational, and executive ability, along with the skill set required to bring large projects to completion.

The potential of this Life Path is not easily expressed, especially in youth. It usually takes many years of hard work and dedication to come to full expression. Few people actualize the full potential of this number early in life and many never achieve it at all. Individuals with the 22 Life Path are most successful when they go outside the common ways of doing things, using their creativity, inspiration, and imagination to find unique ways of achieving their goals. (Read also the description of the 4 Life Path.)

The Birth Day Number

The number of the day on which you were born, included in the calculation of your Life Path number, provides additional information about your nature. It describes particular attributes or talents that you can call on. For example, if you were born on the third of any month, your Birth Day number would be 3; on the twenty-ninth of any month, it would be 2 + 9, or 11 (11/2); on the nineteenth, 1 + 9 = 10, 1 + 0, or 1. Although of lesser importance than the Life Path number, it can provide clues as to which type of career or job would best allow you to manifest your talents. Note in particular if your Birth Day is a Master number, 11 or 22, or a High Energy number, 13, 14, 16, or 19.

1, 10, 19, and 28 Birth Days

If you have a number 1 Birth Day, you strive to be independent and autonomous. You are ambitious, wilful, dynamic, energetic, and forward thinking. At the same time, you are practical and creative, an excellent combination for leadership positions. You have excellent potential for achieving your goals. You are often an inspiration to others. However, 1s, and in particular the 19/1, need to guard against excessive wilfulness and selfishness that can lead to insensitivity to others.

2, 11, 20, and 29 Birth Days

If you have a number 2 Birth Day, you are an excellent mediator and a peacemaker, sensitive to the needs of others. You are the ideal partner and team player. You do well as a healer, teacher and support staff; the power behind the throne. In general, 2s are affectionate and caring, but can be moody and insecure. Also, 11s and 29s (which reduces to 11) exhibit additional sensitivity to the environment as well as a sense of specialness. They will often seek to distinguish themselves in some unique way.

3, 12, 21, and 30 Birth Days

You are generally friendly, loving, caring, enthusiastic, affectionate, and sociable. You are probably creative and imaginative, though you enjoy a practical and hands-on job. You are an excellent communicator and an original thinker, optimistic and energetic. Individuals with 3 Birth Days often do well in the communication, arts, and entertainment fields. You can be scattered, gossipy, and superficial. You may hide your true feelings.

4, 13, 22, and 31 Birth Days

Individuals with 4 Birth Days are excellent organizers, hard workers, conscientious, dedicated, steadfast, structured, rational, and practical. If you have a 4 Birth Day, you can be rigid in your habits and in your thinking, sometimes lacking originality and spontaneity. You work well with routine and order and have a knack for detailed work. The 13 in particular needs to guard against excessive negativity, stubbornness, and rigidity. If your birthday is on the 22nd of the month, you have the additional energies of a Master number, which gives you a desire to make a difference in the world. This is the number of the Master Builder—22s can handle very large undertakings.

5, 14, and 23 Birth Days

If your Birth Day is a 5, you need adventure, variety, change, and lots of freedom to do what you love. You are versatile, a quick learner, original and progressive in your thinking. You generally do not like routine and restriction. You can be impatient and inconsistent. You are an excellent teacher and communicator. If your birthday is on the 14th of the month, you will need to develop patience, order, discipline, and dedication; otherwise, you will find it challenging to achieve your goals.

6, 15, and 24 Birth Days

If you have a 6 Birth Day, you thrive in positions of responsibility. You are a people person, always helpful and attentive to the concerns of others, and are an excellent manager. You are friendly, affectionate, loving, practical, and genuinely caring. You are emotional, and can at times become overly involved in the affairs of others, sometimes meddling. At times, you can be resentful of your responsibilities.

7, 16, and 25 Birth Days

If you have a 7 Birth Day, you enjoy your solitude. You are a deep, analytical thinker and an excellent problem solver. You like mysteries and need to be intellectually challenged. The 16 adds an element of specialness, feelings of being different. Sometimes you can feel superior. In general, 7s can be uncomfortable in emotional situations, and 16s in particular can shy away from intimacy for fear of revealing their true feelings.

8, 17, and 26 Birth Days

If your birthday falls on an 8 day, you have a mind for business and the corporate world may be for you. You have organizational, managerial, administrative, and leadership abilities. Ambitious, energetic, dependable, reliable, focused, and driven, you thrive in a position of power and authority. You have an eye for the big picture and should delegate the detailed work. In your desire to reach your goals, you can be insensitive to others, even lacking in compassion.

9, 18, and 27 Birth Days

If you have a 9 Birth Day, you are generous and kind-hearted, broad-minded, and sensitive to the needs of others—a humanitarian. You are creative and imaginative, and may have artistic abilities. You have great potential for success in the world. You can be emotional and dramatic, sometimes not knowing what to do with your deep feelings. At times, you can be overly generous, and may become resentful when your giving is not returned in kind.

Your Future Starts Now

Before we get into the business of mapping out future trends, you may want to pause and reflect on your current situation. A prerequisite to making effective decisions for the future is that you first acknowledge where you have come from, recognize how you arrived at your present circumstances, and then take stock of where you are in your life at the moment. Past decisions and actions determined where you are now, and your present and upcoming decisions will determine your future. The more you know and accept yourself, the more likely you will be to make decisions that will reflect your true desires and ultimately take your life in the direction of personal fulfillment.

With your Life Path and Birth Day numbers, you are probably beginning to have a much clearer picture of your journey. For example, if you have a number 4 Life Path, you may have a tendency to make decisions based on material insecurity and fear of scarcity. No matter how bright your trends for the future, you are likely to take a moderate approach to rising opportunities. If, on the other hand you are strongly marked by the number 5's need for freedom and change, you may experience frustration and limitation during a period of number 4 energy.

Being aware of past behaviours, you can modify your approach, leading to better opportunities and results. This way, you are better equipped to take on the challenges and opportunities presented by an upcoming trend, thus actively participating in the creation of a better future for yourself. In the previous example, addressing your material insecurity and fear of scarcity issues by taking appropriate measures such as sitting down with an advisor and laying out a financial plan, perhaps combined with a positive mindset, may prepare you to rise to greater, bolder challenges in the future. You could then take advantage of excellent opportunities for growth, which you might otherwise have avoided.

Perhaps you have a job, maybe even a good job by today's market standards, but you feel somehow limited, unhappy with your present occupation and are clueless as to where to go next. You have a sense of having missed opportunities, or that something is lacking in your life. You don't know where to turn, or how long your present situation of loss and confusion will last.

Entrepreneurs approach obstacles and challenges differently from the average working person. I have found that the charts of

CHAPTER 2 · YOUR PERSONAL LIFE ROADMAP

entrepreneurs tend to include more challenges than the charts of people who are comfortably employed. On the one hand, these challenges offer more possibilities for growth, while on the other hand, more chances of staying blocked. Even if they find themselves in the wrong business, as happens many times with a first attempt at entrepreneurship, there is usually a positive outcome from the experience, such as an important lesson learned about one's abilities, limits, unique skills, and capabilities.

Many are quitting their jobs of twenty-plus years and venturing into the world of entrepreneurship. Many of these people know themselves well, they know what they like, they know what they want, and they know what they are good at. They also know what they don't like and don't want, but not always what they are not good at. They generally think they can do it all. Although the prospect of jumping into an uncertain world can appear frightening, they stand on the confidence of past experience and acquired knowledge, a powerful force that fuels them forward. It takes a fair amount of courage to make the leap from the security of a job to the uncertain world of the self-employed.

Today's job market is fiercely competitive. It is all the more important that the individual ensures that they are employing their best assets in their job. People perform best when they are doing what they are good at. The employee, in comparison to the self-employed worker, has a different set of challenges to address when considering matters such as life purpose, direction, and personal growth and satisfaction. They must manage their life and goals within the context of the company or organization for which they work. Their efforts are often under-appreciated or even not recognized by their superiors, who are themselves overwhelmed by responsibilities and stresses of their own.

The employee must derive satisfaction by setting personal goals and recognizing their own worth within those of the group culture. There are times when the employee realizes that their goals are no longer in alignment with the values of the company. They may force themselves to fit into this now-foreign environment, sometimes for years, setting into motion a pattern of negative growth and dissatisfaction. Many employees leave their jobs because the stress of working in an unsuitable environment has taken its toll. This can manifest as a burnout or other health-related issue, or marital breakdown, and often both. Seldom is poor performance on the job the initial cause.

Now, with the knowledge of your Life Path and Birth Day numbers, you are beginning to lay down the foundation for mapping out your life journey. This knowledge will help you make choices that are more appropriate, given your particular talents, abilities, and inclinations. You may belong to the significant number of people who are not living the life of their dreams, who experience a feeling of something missing in their lives, or who have some level of unmet hopes and expectations. No matter your situation, keeping your numbers in mind, ask yourself a few questions to shed light on where you are before we look at upcoming trends and start to plan where you are going next.

- Is my job/career satisfactory? If not, why not?
- How do I define success for myself?
- Have I attained the goals I set out for myself many years ago?
- Am I tending to all the important areas of my life? If not, which are being ignored, and why? Which are outdated? Why am I holding onto outdated activities?
- What are my long-term goals for myself? My family? My business? My retirement?
- On a scale of one to ten, how would I rate my life overall at this time?
- If I could wave a magic wand, what would I change in my life?
- Do my lifestyle and career reflect the potential of my Life Path and Birth Day numbers? If not, what could I do to be more in tune with the energies of my numbers?

CHAPTER 2 • YOUR PERSONAL LIFE ROADMAP

In the Company of Numbers

A fun way of understanding the characteristics of the numbers is to lay them out in a company setting, assigning the most suitable jobs for each of the numbers. If the numbers were people, where would you find them in a large company?

Number 1

The 1 is highly energized, self-motivated, autonomous, and independent. It is the number of the entrepreneur, the self-starter, the consultant, and can do well in a self-employed capacity. In the context of a company, since they pretty much prefer to be their own boss, they are likely to be found heading up their own department, or at least enjoying being project starters. The 1 says "starters" because they are quick to move on to new projects. Their enthusiasm and energy can be an inspiration for others, and so can make very good team trainers and group leaders.

Number 2

The 2 is relational, sensitive, and receptive, as well as discreet and discerning. They are the listeners, counsellors, coaches, mentors, peacekeepers, and make excellent support staff, and do well in human resources and customer relations. Because they do not seek glory for themselves, the 2 is the perfect "right-hand person." The 2 is also an excellent negotiator and mediator. Because they are able to step back and get a sense of the driving forces behind interactions, they have the ability to moderate and temper situations that might otherwise be difficult to manage.

Number 3

The 3 is sociable, talkative, and likes to be on the go. The 3 is the artist, the creative mind, the entertainer, the communicator. They can do very well in sales, and may even enjoy being on the road. They can also excel in marketing and communications. They generally have likeable personalities and can get along with just about anyone; they are wonderful in a reception post. They are excellent at organizing seminars, travel plans, meetings and conferences, and especially event planning.

Number 4

The 4 is the worker bee: hard-working, organized, and well-suited for the day-to-day operations of the company. Dependable and reliable, they find value in order, routine, and stable structure. They are drawn to administration, clerical, filing, data management, bookkeeping, budgeting, and accounting positions, the very foundation on which the company stands. With experience, they can rise to become invaluable assets in organizational and operations management.

Number 5

The 5 is the number of freedom; it is the pioneer, the adventurer and does not do well in confining environments. They are the "Jack of all trades." They have a low threshold for boredom and need room to grow, explore and expand; they generally avoid routine 9-to-5 jobs. Innovative, experimental, and progressive by nature, they are well suited for the research and development (R&D) department. They are the oddballs in jeans and running shoes blowing stuff up in the lab downstairs causing grief for the accounting department upstairs. (Speaking from personal experience, as I worked as an R&D tech-writer for a few years. Not surprisingly, I have two 14/5s in my core numbers!)

Number 6

The 6 is all about cooperation, harmony, health, and balance; it is highly socialized and interactive, and is a natural for management positions. Being sensitive to the needs of all concerned, they excel in human relations and are perfect for heading up the human resources department. Individuals with a strong number 6 signature are great at developing and coordinating workflow, and stimulating and supporting teamwork. They are capable of ensuring that employee needs as well as company objectives are met.

Number 7

The 7 is solitary in nature, a thinker, and an excellent problem solver. They excel at complex analysis, whether business, market, operations, or product development, as well as strategic planning, research, or even industrial spying. They fulfill the research half of R&D. They are born educators, and can develop effective training programs for employees as well as clients. They can also be excellent therapists. The 7s work well on their own, actually preferring a fair amount of solitude, and require little supervision. They are discreet and can be entrusted with sensitive matters.

Number 8

The 8 is a powerhouse; the visionary, the one with the big idea, the one who aims for success, the person in charge. The 8 is upper management material: CEO, CFO, and directors of the company. They aim for the top, thriving in positions of power and authority, never shying away from a challenge that will take them one step closer to their goals. While in the top spot, the wise ones will call on the 6s and 2s to coordinate with all the departments to make things run smoothly and efficiently. With well-chosen managers and visionaries in place, each number easily finds their unique function.

Number 9

The 9 is multi-talented and complex, and can fill many roles. They may gravitate toward positions that involve travel, negotiation, export, trade, foreign affairs, or diplomacy. They have a strong humanitarian side, and will opt for the good of everyone before seeking glory for themselves. They do well in functions that serve the community and the world at large as well as activities that enhance the corporate image such as fundraising activities, new economic models, and environmental initiatives.

As a perfect example, my dad was an electrical engineer, with an expertise in a niche field. He turned down several management positions so he could continue to travel the world and share his knowledge. He even learned how to read, write, and speak Japanese in his 50s. He also decided to learn to play flamenco on the guitar after a trip to Spain. The number 9 at its best!

CHAPTER 3

The 9-Year Epicycle

Mapping the Journey

Effective planning and goal setting has become one of the key ingredients in all success formulas. Making lists of short- and long-term goals and creating picture books are among some of the popular tools for those wanting to have a more hands-on approach to attracting success and abundance into their lives. Being aware of your numerology cycles *in addition* to goal setting, planning, coaching, positive habits, etc., will greatly enhance your chances of success. As stated in the previous chapter, your Life Path number establishes the foundation for your journey, setting the general tone of the opportunities and experiences you are likely to encounter along the way. Having been introduced to your Life Path, you can now begin to map out the details of your journey.

In this chapter, we will focus on the second set of numbers derived from your date of birth, the numbers concerned with the short- to mid-term trends found in the 9-Year Epicycle. These are the most exciting and powerful numbers to work with in planning and goal setting as they describe events, circumstances, situations, lessons, and challenges encountered on a yearly, monthly, and daily basis. The 9-Year Epicycle maps out the details of your journey. These numbers include: the Personal Year, the Personal Month, and the Personal Day.

The 9-Year Epicycle, also known as the Personal Year Cycle, is a powerful tool not only for establishing an effective long-term plan, but also for gauging your growth and accomplishment levels over time. This cycle is broken down into individual years, from 1 to 9, each with its own energies and tendencies, called the Personal Year numbers. The years are then considered on a month-by-month basis, again each with its own numerical value from 1 to 9, giving us the Personal Month numbers. Finally, for added information, you can include Personal Day numbers for daily trends.

The cycle begins with a number 1 Personal Year, a time of renewed energy and new beginnings. From the 1 Year, the cycle progresses and develops through each year until it reaches its peak at the 8 Personal Year, at which point the rewards of the efforts of the past seven years are reaped. The cycle winds down with the 9 Year, a period of rest and release, ideally a sabbatical, during which, time should be spent finishing off projects, integrating learning and slowing down activity, thus clearing the way for the next epicycle beginning the following year.

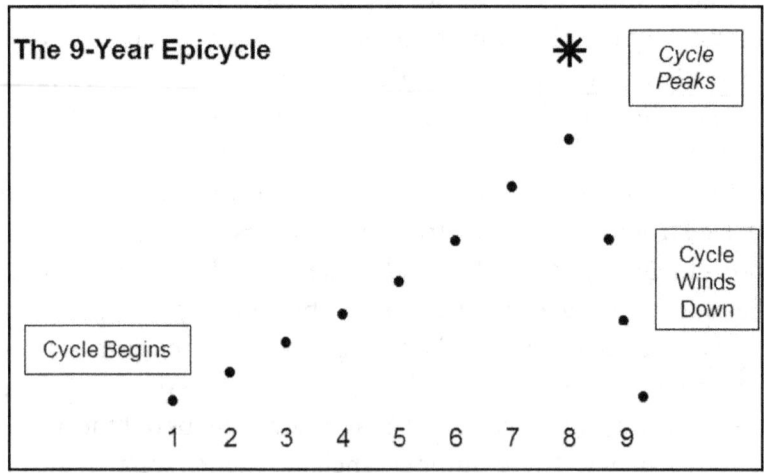

If you are in the first three years of an epicycle, you are in the early planning and development stage, and can focus on

CHAPTER 3 · THE 9-YEAR EPICYCLE

establishing a new direction on which to build long-term goals. This is the time to explore, experiment, consider your options, and expand into new horizons. In other words, you have the benefit of time on your side.

In the middle stage, the fourth, fifth, and sixth years, plans and projects should be well underway and solidly established. You are now in the thick of it, and should focus on doing whatever it takes so that you can attain tangible results. Make any necessary adjustments, establish a practical system or method, and focus on the work at hand.

During the final three years of the cycle, you should concentrate on bringing your projects to a close. This is not the time to quit; you are close to the finish line now. You may be inclined to look ahead toward where you want to go next and begin to consider your next set of long-term goals. Take the time to finish things off first. You are running out of time as your current cycle winds down to a close. If you have been working with specific goals in mind and hope to experience success, now is the time to hunker down and give it all you've got. Although time is running out, you now have the benefit of experience on your side.

The 3 Stages of The 9-Year Epicycle

Initiate, Renew, Develop			Build, Grow, Consolidate			Achieve, Integrate, Conclude		
1	2	3	4	5	6	7	8	9

If you are reaching the end of your epicycle and realize that you are far from achieving the goals you set for yourself years earlier, you may want to consider making adjustments. Trim back the fat. Aim for more realistic goals, so that in the end, you will experience a certain degree of satisfaction. If you have aimed too high, you could end up feeling frustrated or discouraged should you fail to achieve your goals, reinforcing negative attitudes about your ability to be successful. Coming from a place of failure, it will make it all the more difficult for you to set new goals once your next cycle begins. It's better for your confidence and self-esteem to successfully achieve a lesser goal than to aim for and fail at a larger one. By consistently setting realistic goals that reflect where you are on your journey, you will experience your life as a series of successes rather than failed attempts. Don't be like those who spend a long life in waiting for success to miraculously happen. You are the one who can make it happen!

The 9-Year Epicycle has a beginning phase motivated by a sense of optimism, new possibilities, and opportunities; a productive middle phase filled with work, expansion, and responsibility; and a final third phase of accomplishment, rewards, and completion. By keeping the natural progression of the 9-Year Epicycle in mind when establishing goals, your projects will flow more smoothly and you will feel less challenged by obstacles and delays. You will feel more in control and more confident, things will work better, and you will view most situations from a realistic perspective.

The Personal Year Number

The Personal Year number can be used as a sort of signpost along the road, indicating road conditions, curves, bumps, and points of interest for the part of your journey that lasts for the duration of one calendar year. The manner in which one person experiences a certain set of circumstances may be different from another's experience of the same. It is therefore important to base your interpretations and decisions on your personal life journey as well as on your present level of learning and life experience rather than on a generalized formula. When interpreting meanings for your trends, remember to apply them to your personal context. Your life will not suddenly change course and turn into someone else's journey just because your trends have changed. If, for example, you have determined that the number 2 is a prominent

CHAPTER 3 • THE 9-YEAR EPICYCLE

factor in your life, but the energy of the number 1 is lacking, it does not mean that because you are in a number 1 Personal Year all of a sudden you will become daring, adventurous, and independent. You could in fact feel a bit nervous in a 1 Personal Year, facing the uncertainty of new opportunities.

Also keep in mind that not all days, months, and years contain events of major importance in our lives. Sometimes, several forgettable years can pass by before anything of importance occurs. Numbers do not define with absolute certainty the nature and outcome of every event, nor do they predict with fated certainty the result of all your decisions. The various cycles described by your numbers indicate likely tendencies, lessons to be learned, and potential trends. Whether or not you are comfortable with the energy of a particular number will determine how you will deal with it when it becomes active in your life.

Calculating the Personal Year Number

To calculate the Personal Year number for a given year, first reduce the numbers of the Birth Day, Birth Month, and Year to a single digit. Note that if the result is either 11 or 22, do not reduce to a single digit. There may also be a High Energy number in the result. For example, for a person with a birthday on June 29, you would calculate the Personal Year number for 2026 as follows:

Birth Month	6	6	6	6
Birth Day	29	2+9	11	11
Calendar Year*	2026	1	1	1
			18	9

*2026 is reduced: 2 + 0 + 2 + 6 = 10, reduces to 1.

Note that if you choose to use the Master numbers 11 and 22 as Personal Year numbers, some of the results for Personal Months and Personal Days will be different. This will be evident with 11/2 and 22/4 years. Not all numerologists use the Master numbers for the Personal Year calculations. I personally find that they can add a bit of extra depth to the period in question. Feel free to try them to see how they work for you.

Also, as this cycle is based on the calendar year, the Personal Year begins in January and ends in December. For detailed descriptions as well as yearly planning exercises for each Personal Year, see Chapters 4–12.

The Personal Month Number

The Personal Month number provides helpful information for planning your year on a month-by-month basis. It will not change or significantly modify the trends indicated by your Personal Year number, but it will help focus its energy into productive areas of activity. To calculate a Personal Month, add the Calendar Month, reduced to a single digit or Master number to the Personal Year number. For example, the Personal Month for December, for a person whose Personal Year is 8:

Current Personal Year	8	8	8
Calendar Month	12	1+2	3
			11/2

For the interpretation of your Personal Months, for added depth, you can consider Master numbers as well as High Energy numbers. The energy of the Personal Month begins on the first of the month and ends on the last day. Its energy peaks in the two middle weeks of the month and wanes in the last few days. The Personal Months can be interpreted as scaled down versions of Personal Years.

As you will notice from the following table, the 6, 7, 8, and 9 Personal Years each contain a complete nine-month cycle. These years are important in that they are a time when much accomplishment is possible. When you have reached the 6 Personal Year, initial research, study and preliminary work will very likely

CHAPTER 3 • THE 9-YEAR EPICYCLE

have been completed, and you will want to focus the bulk of your energies on completing projects and attaining goals.

Personal Year Number

	1	2	3	4	5	6	7	8	9
Jan	2	3	4	5	6	7	8	9	1
Feb	3	4	5	6	7	8	9	1	2
Mar	4	5	6	7	8	9	1	2	3
Apr	5	6	7	8	9	1	2	3	4
May	6	7	8	9	1	2	3	4	5
June	7	8	9	1	2	3	4	5	6
July	8	9	1	2	3	4	5	6	7
Aug	9	1	2	3	4	5	6	7	8
Sep	1	2	3	4	5	6	7	8	9
Oct	2	3	4	5	6	7	8	9	1
Nov	3	4	5	6	7	8	9	1	2
Dec	4	5	6	7	8	9	1	2	3

Personal Month Numbers

Note that September is more than just "back to school" as it carries the same number signature as the current year. If you play around with the math, you will notice that the number 9 disappears in any calculation. For example, 4 + 9 = 13, which reduces to 4 (1 + 3). September can be intense, as yearly projects and issues can come to the fore.

If September is the same number as the current year, it means that October will be the following number. I call October the "preview" month, as it carries the energy of the next year. You might get some ideas for what you want to do in the next year. But first, focus on finishing the current year.

Vacation Planning by the Numbers

Numerology is a phenomenal tool for planning personal and professional activities, and knowing your Personal Month number can be helpful for choosing the vacation that best suits your state of mind and energy level. Overall, you will find that when making choices that are in harmony with your cycles, life will unfold more smoothly. You may not always have the choice of when to take your vacation, but you can choose how to spend your time.

You may wonder which is more important: the Personal Year or Personal Month number. The Personal Year number sets the tone for the entire year, so it represents a trend of primary importance. The Personal Month number sets the tone for a shorter period and should be evaluated within the context of the Personal Year. Much like a few days of mild weather might occur in the middle of winter, the prevailing season is still winter. Keep the big picture in mind alongside the smaller picture.

Personal Month 1

You are charged up and ready to start new projects this month, and a vacation may not be the first thing on your mind. Your energy level is high and you are ready for action. You're more inclined to do things independently and start projects on your own at this time. If you can manage a vacation, it's not likely to be a sitting-on-the-dock-of-the-bay variety; more of a climb-the-highest-mountain variety. You're on the move and ready to go; your travel partner will have to be prepared to keep up with you!

Personal Month 2

The 2 is responsive and receptive by nature, and so quieter than the 1. You will enjoy connecting with friends, engaging in activities and projects with others, reaching out, helping others, or reaching out for help for a project that is dear to you (as long as it's not work-related!). It's okay to slow down, enjoy life, and deepen relationships now. You're probably not inclined to spend too much time alone this month, so finding ways to interact and share with others will be very rewarding. This is a great time for a romantic getaway, especially a honeymoon, or a renewal of vows, or maybe a proposal!

CHAPTER 3 • THE 9-YEAR EPICYCLE

Personal Month 3

The 3 is social, energetic, and fun-loving by nature, so a 3 Personal Month is a great time for a vacation. Take advantage of this upbeat and joyful 3 trend to expand your social circle and generally have a good time. Go dancing, catch some shows, do activities that take your mind off work. If so inclined, engage in artistic or creative activities. Be aware that a bit of planning might make your vacation more efficient; the 3 can be a little distracting. You may want to make a budget before going on vacation; otherwise, you'll spend the next few months paying for it. Remember to enjoy yourself!

Personal Month 4

If you must take a vacation in a 4 Personal Month, you may find it difficult to justify taking the time off when there is so much work to be done. All the more reason to take some time out to rest, relax, and take a break from all that hard work. You might prefer a family vacation over an exotic and expensive getaway. You may find the break you need by puttering around the house, attending to odds and ends, spending time in the kitchen, in the garden, or on a fun home renovation project. The important point is to take some time away from your regular job.

Personal Month 5

You are ready for adventure and primed to try new things this month. You are likely to sense a need for freedom and an aversion to being trapped indoors. Choose activities that break you out of your everyday routine; do something completely different. Head for open spaces, escape rigid schedules and obligations. Although some of your experiences may be temporary in nature, the well-deserved freedom and adventure will help push back some of your boundaries, leaving you free to experience more of your unfolding.

Personal Month 6

You're in the ideal mode for a nice vacation with family and friends. You have much to share with others, so don't be surprised if you are asked to help out in some way. Don't take on so much responsibility that you have little time left to pamper yourself; practise setting boundaries. Plan a classy outing, go for a makeover, buy some fabulous new clothes; enjoy a concert or an art show. You want to feel good about yourself, and you want to look great. Make sure there is peace, harmony, and balance in your life this month. Let things unfold without the need to manage every detail; it's vacation time, not management time.

Personal Month 7

You may be more inclined to stay home and hibernate this month then go on a fancy cruise with friends. The 7 is quiet and reflective, appropriate for deep thinking, problem solving, learning, or simply catching up on some non-work-related reading or research. If you must schedule a vacation at this time, make sure you will have some quiet time for yourself, or, if you have a travel partner, choose quiet, simple activities that you both enjoy. This is a great time for a retreat and especially for spending time in nature. If you want a fun activity, try puzzles. The 7 is great at problem solving.

Personal Month 8

You're at the top of your game this month, and more focused on career, finances, and getting ahead in the world than on trivialities. If you can get away from work long enough, or if you must take your vacation this month—and that's a big if—you may be open to a luxury vacation. You've worked hard, and now you want a taste of the best that life has to offer. Save your pennies well in advance for this vacation; it will be worth it! Again, that's if you can tear yourself away from your business and career obligations.

CHAPTER 3 • THE 9-YEAR EPICYCLE

Personal Month 9

The 9 is associated with completion, endings, and closure. It's time to wrap things up and let go. It can be an excellent time for a vacation that is focused on rest and relaxation. Treat yourself to a nice spa getaway; it's the perfect time to recharge your batteries. If you don't have the energy for a getaway, engage in a little decluttering and drop off what you don't need at your local thrift store. This will help make room for new experiences, just around the corner. While enjoying some relaxation time, what seem like great ideas might emerge. Being more suitable for winding down, this is not the best time to start new projects; let your great new ideas settle for a while, wait for your number 1 month to get started on anything new.

The Personal Day Number

For added insights on a day-to-day basis, consider your Personal Day number. While this number may seem less significant than the Personal Year and Month numbers, being aware of it can help with the planning and organizing of your weekly activities. To calculate your Personal Day number, add the values—reduced to single digits or Master numbers—of your Personal Year, the Calendar Month, and Calendar Day. In the example below for February 14, for a person whose Personal Year is 7:

Current Personal Year	7	7	7
Calendar Month	2	2	2
Calendar Day	14	1+4	5
			14/5

In this example, there is a High Energy number behind the Personal Day number, 14. If this was your number for this day and a friend had set you up on a dinner date, your Valentine's evening would probably not turn out as you expected! The 14/5 typically brings change, unexpected events, and surprises.

Interpretations for Personal Days are similar to those for Personal Months and Personal Years, but should be scaled down to a day-to-day level of activity. Before interpreting a Personal Day number, keep in mind your global yearly picture, that is, your Personal Year number, as well as your monthly trends as indicated by your Personal Month number. Also keep in mind your potential as indicated by your Life Path and Birth Day numbers, and your relationship to the numbers. Note High Energy influences. The following interpretations are meant as suggestions to help you determine the nature of the energy of the day. Use the keywords to interpret your days according to your needs, personality, and lifestyle.

1 (19/1) Personal Day

This is a good time to begin new activities, to look for a new job, or start a new project. You feel bold, confident, and ready to express initiative, take action, and get the gears in motion. This is your time. You could be feeling ambitious, creative, and energetic. You may be inclined to do things by yourself today. Beware of a tendency to see things from your point of view alone, and in the process, ignoring the needs of others. If a 19/1 Day, try not to be overly pushy with your plans. It isn't worth stepping on other people's toes to get what you want.

2 (11/2) Personal Day

Be receptive and wait for feedback from the world around you before making important decisions. Gather information, reach out and touch base with leads and important contacts. Avoid conflict and misunderstandings. This is a good day for a romantic tête-à-tête. You may want to pay particular attention to the needs of others, employ tact and diplomacy. Be a good listener, partner, or companion. You could be more sensitive, or intuitive than usual if this is an 11/2 Day. Take advantage of the 11/2 energy and connect with your Higher Self, or your Guides.

CHAPTER 3 • THE 9-YEAR EPICYCLE

3 Personal Day

This is a great day for scheduling social and fun events, dinner parties, and outings with friends. Focus on communications, return those phone calls you've been putting off, or work on a creative project. Schedule brainstorming sessions with colleagues or your team; work on your network of contacts. You may be feeling optimistic and positive, but could be a little disorganized or scattered today. Leave the day open; find avenues of creative self-expression. Have a good laugh, dress up, and enjoy a night on the town.

4 (13/4, 22/4) Personal Day

Apply yourself to the details of the day, stick to routine, and focus on the tasks at hand. Focus on those projects that have been sitting on your desk, blocking progress in other areas of your work. Take care of accounting, bookkeeping, filing, or organizing your workspace. Spend time with family. Do household chores, grocery shopping, pantry inventory, home projects, renovations, or heavy physical work. Maybe bake your favourite cake! If this is a 13/4 Day, you may be frustrated with the amount of work that seems to have piled up in front of you. If it is a 22/4 Day, you may feel pressed to get things accomplished.

5 (14/5) Personal Day

Expect changes to your plans, or unexpected or surprise occurrences. This is a good day for adventure, new experiences, and travel, and for promoting yourself or expanding your business. You won't be very interested in doing paperwork and tedious tasks today. Give yourself a little room to breathe. Be flexible. Have fun in the kitchen; test a new recipe. If a 14/5, don't expect things to go as planned; the day is likely to be more hectic than you would like. Expect surprises or upsets. Guard against a tendency to be impatient, to overindulge, or to avoid responsibility.

6 Personal Day

Take care of family business and pay attention to loved ones today. You will need to establish some measure of balance in your life after yesterday's hectic pace. Increased demands may be made on your time and energy, and you will be very much appreciated as you tend to your responsibilities. Keep in mind that it's okay to set boundaries for yourself. Plan a romantic dinner, a family gathering, or an activity that will give you a sense of peace and harmony. This is a great day to attend a live concert!

7 (16/7) Personal Day

You may feel inclined to take some quiet time out for yourself. Reflect, meditate, read, or take a spa day. This is a good time for intellectual activities, research, and study. Avoid excessive stress and confrontation. Do some serious thinking; review your monthly plan. Go for a long walk in the woods, listen to music, spend some quiet time in the garden, or on a hobby. This isn't a good day for planning a social event. If a 16/7 Day, it may be best to avoid complicated personal relationships. You could take things personally, or feel misunderstood.

8 Personal Day

Deal with money, power, and career issues now. This is a good day for finances, business, price shopping, or making important purchases. You are feeling empowered, driven to achieve your goals, maybe even fearless, and at the top of your game. Schedule that important business meeting, or make business decisions. Your confidence level is high, and you believe in your ability to achieve your goals. It's time to show what you're made of.

9 Personal Day

This is a good day to finish off projects, clean up your office or home, and try to unwind. This is not the best time to start new projects or to commit to long-term plans. Spend the day outdoors, enjoying nature, go for a drive in the country, or take in an art show or exhibition. Get some rest. Do something for others; participate in a community event or fundraiser. Follow-up on messages and phone calls; have lunch with friends. Release all grievances and anxieties. Be generous. Give of yourself. This is a good day for a public appearance.

Exercise: Key Life Sectors

In preparation for using the knowledge of the numbers effectively, it is important that you know where and how to invest your time and energy. The following exercise can be helpful in identifying Key Life Sectors, those areas of life that you feel are important, based on your values, in which you feel you should be devoting time and energy. It is similar to the Identifying Roles approach used by Stephen Covey in his Habit 3: Putting First Things First (*The 7 Habits of Highly Effective People*). As an aid to defining your Key Life Sectors, consider the following questions. Then, list your Key Life Sectors.

- What is most important in my life?
- What do I value the most?
- If I could do only one thing in my life, what would that be?
- What can I not live without?
- What do I need more of in my life?
- What did I dream of doing when I was young?
- What makes me smile?
- What gives me energy?
- What am I passionate about?
- What do I love to talk about with friends?
- What makes me jump out of bed in the morning?
- How would I like to spend my time?
- What do I believe I should be working on?
- Where do I feel the most useful to others?

- When am I the most appreciated by others?
- What is that one thing I would do if only I had time?
- What do I plan to do when I retire?
- What do I want to do more of?

Look for patterns in your answers. If you consistently answered that you would like to have more fun at work, at home, when you retire, one day when you have more time, or when you were young, you dreamed of being an entertainer, then perhaps you have a deep and unanswered need for lightening up a bit. Maybe you should consider finding an outlet for self-expression. You may have a long-buried number 3 influence somewhere, the number of the arts and entertainment. Take this need seriously, and make time for an activity that would allow it in your life—if not on a daily basis, then at least on a weekly basis. You might consider joining an improv group or community theatre.

Some example Key Life Sectors:
- Self/personal development
- Family, spouse, parents
- Friends, social activities
- Health, fitness
- Boss, manager, employee
- Business development
- Professional development, career
- Creativity, self-expression
- Community involvement/sharing
- Home projects
- Fun time

Make a list of the five or six Key Life Sectors that are most important to you. These are the areas of life in which you will be devoting time and energy. Try to establish a healthy balance between the personal and professional sectors. Sometimes, simply re-establishing equilibrium in your life is sufficient to release much accumulated stress. A number 6 Year or Month is a great time for establishing balance.

Be reasonable in your choice of areas of activity. Choosing too many areas of focus can lead to failure, as you will be less likely to meet your objectives. It is best to focus on fewer areas for now, adding to your list later, as you master your time and ability to plan. You cannot do it all at the same time. Accept this fact and you will find that much stress magically disappears! Also, your list of Key Life Sectors will change as the demands of your life and your lifestyle change. By remaining open and flexible, you will always be doing the things you feel are right for you at any given moment.

Exercise: My Personal History

Another very interesting exercise that you will find most helpful is to go back in time and review the events of your life as though it were a movie. Make a list, year by year, if you can, of not only the important events, but also the quiet times, the apparently insignificant periods of your life. Calculate the Personal Year numbers for those years that contain important events, such as a move, the start of a job, the end of a job, the start and end of school, or the start or end of an important relationship. You will probably identify recurring cycles in your life.

This exercise will give you an excellent idea of what to expect the next time a particular Personal Year comes around. If you have a number 3 Life Path, for example, you may find that 6 Personal Years have been very productive times for professional and social activities. From this exercise, you may recognize relationship, financial, or career trends. Refer to your Personal History as you read the descriptions of the Personal Years in the following chapters.

CHAPTER 4

The 1 Personal Year

Working With the Personal Years

The following chapters will provide more detailed descriptions of each of the 9 Personal Years. Additionally, the trends for the Personal Months that are unique to each year will be illustrated. Note that the descriptions for the Personal Years and Personal Months are to be used as guidelines for determining possible scenarios for setting goals that reflect your values, needs, and desires at a given time in your life. Use the keywords from Chapter 1 to interpret potential trends as they may apply to you. You can also use words that resonate better with you. Each person is unique, and each has a unique relationship with the numbers. Also keep in mind that the Personal Month numbers are secondary to the Personal Year numbers, and should be considered along with your other primary numbers.

At the end of each chapter, you will find 2 exercises: Exercise 1: Preparing for Your Personal Year, and Exercise 2: Year-End Review. You may find these exercises helpful for making the best use of the opportunities and trends for the year. The Year-End Review exercise will also help to add confidence and clear vision as you track the progress of your unique journey on a monthly and yearly basis.

Renewal, New Beginnings, Rebirth

The 1 Personal Year is a time of new beginnings, a time for making adjustments to your life journey, especially if you feel that you have veered off course. This could be an important crossroads. It is a key year in that it is the one time when you can effectively break away from the past and set your life in a completely new direction. Now is the time to abandon old patterns and launch those new projects you've been dreaming of and planning for so long. If you are in a position that is right for you, a field that allows you to grow and develop your personal potential, this will be the ideal time to take the next big step forward.

Make the adjustments in your personal and professional life that will eventually enable you to pursue those activities that most closely reflect your values and goals. If you are in a job or situation that you dislike or that does not allow you to grow as you would like, then this may be the time to make some changes. You can now steer yourself in a new area of activity, if this is what is required to make your life more fulfilling. The 1 Personal Year allows you to make radical changes and break from the past.

Note your response to the "My Experience with the Number 1" exercise from Chapter 1. How you relate to this energy will in part determine your experience of the 1 Personal Year. Autonomy, independence, self-reliance, initiative, and a strong sense of self will contribute to the success of your new endeavours. This is the time to take care of *you*. Focus on your life purpose, your values, your desires, and your goals. If in the past you have been shy, inhibited, reserved, or reluctant to take advantage of opportunities for advancement, you may try being more assertive and bold now. New opportunities are likely to come your way. You could be offered a position in an entirely different field of work, or you may have an opening in a new location. Significant life transitions are common in a 1 Personal Year.

Re-evaluate your long-term plan, personally and professionally. If you haven't defined one yet, now would be the time to do

CHAPTER 4 · THE 1 PERSONAL YEAR

so. Consider projects that could take a few years to complete. You have time on your side now. There is less pressure to reach your goals now as you are just at the beginning of the cycle. This is the time to transform your dreams, aspirations, hopes, and intentions into reality. It is time to take action. A positive attitude and a bit of courage will help you overcome the obstacles that have previously prevented you from making significant changes in your life. Be bold and confident.

Embrace change and adventure. Move forward with fresh, new, and innovative ideas. More importantly, address the challenges of your particular Life Path. Take initiative and practise healthy assertiveness while maintaining respect for others. This is your key to success for the entire year. If you are ready to retire or reduce your workload, again, this is the time to set the new pace. It is up to you to carve out a path with a new future for yourself.

You may already be engaged in activities that reflect well your talents and abilities, and feel no need to make major adjustments at this time in your life. It is not necessary to change your direction each time you reach a 1 Personal Year. However, it is important to undertake something new in a 1 Personal Year, even if it doesn't lead to any major professional or career changes. Learning something new can be both invigorating and empowering. Undertaking new activities prevents you from becoming overly entrenched in old ways of doing things, opens up your creative energies, gives added confidence, and facilitates progress. Tackling new challenges and opportunities favours flexibility, which makes it easier to make changes and adjustments as they arise.

During a 1 Personal Year, it is not uncommon to feel alone, sometimes lost or unsupported, unsure about whether or not you are doing the right thing. It can be frightening to face the future with little reassurance or guarantee that your projects will work out. Practise tuning into your intuition; be open to receiving inner guidance. People in your immediate environment may feel threatened as you begin to move in a new direction. Others will not always agree with your new ideas and plans, and may not be supportive as you move forward with your life. Most people resist change. The old "If it ain't broke, don't fix it" approach is rather well entrenched in our way of thinking.

Sometimes, change can be interpreted as a signal that something was previously wrong, inadequate, or somehow unsatisfactory. Often, this is actually the case. When a person suddenly makes a decision to move in an entirely new direction, those who are close may wonder if they have done something wrong. Your decision for change may cause them to question their own way of doing things. Change can be unsettling, even threatening. The best policy is to make certain that your decision is based on your inner guidance, and to not placate others with excuses or elaborate reasons for your decision. People will eventually accept your choices when they see that you are in a far better place for it. They may even support you in your endeavours at a later date. Everyone loves a champion, and following the voice of your heart will allow you to be the champion of your life.

At the same time, be mindful of those people in your life who might feel neglected as you focus on yourself this year. Keep the lines of communication open. Reassure loved ones that you will not abandon them. Share your great new ideas with the special ones who are there to support you during times of change and transition. Know that you are never alone.

Natalie, a 19/1 Life Path, began to dance when she was just 3 years old. When she reached her mid-teens, a doctor informed her that her hip joints and knees were permanently damaged, and that she should consider other career options. Devastated, she cried for months. But in typical 19/1 Life Path fashion, she pulled herself up and declared that she would rather try and fail than to never have given herself a chance. She graduated from high school in a special dance program in the spring of a 9 Personal Year. In the fall of that same year, she began her first session at college, but for some strange reason, was compelled to

CHAPTER 4 · THE 1 PERSONAL YEAR

enrol in the pure and applied science program. In a 9 Personal Year, as you will see in Chapter 12, it's not uncommon to become distracted and veer off track. "If ever I need these courses," she reasoned, "I'll have them."

The following January, now in a 1 Personal Year, at the start of a new epicycle, she switched out of pure and applied science and moved to communications, making the adjustment toward a more appropriate direction, given her lifelong interest in dance. (Note that there was no dance program at her college, otherwise this would have been her choice.) By the end of that 9-Year Epicycle, Natalie had successfully completed college, obtained a Bachelor of Fine Arts in contemporary dance at university and a postgraduate degree in Fine Arts Management, completed a series of certificates in Pilates training, and established a successful business as a freelance dance teacher and Pilates instructor. The following year, a 1 Personal Year, and the start of a new epicycle, she began developing ideas for a new approach that would integrate dance and Pilates. If you aren't exhausted just reading this, keep in mind that all the while, she worked two to three part-time jobs to pay for school and rent! Natalie's journey reflects well the drive, energy, initiative, creativity, and autonomy of the 19/1 Life Path.

For some people, especially those needing a significant life makeover, things don't always become clear until the later months, September or October, of the 1 Personal Year. Don't panic if you haven't gotten a clear picture of your life direction on the first day of January. At the same time, it is important to take some initiative in a 1 Personal Year, so as to engage the energy of the new epicycle. Even if things are still unclear by the end of the year, do try something new, even if it is only a small step. Also keep in mind that it can take the first two to three years of the new epicycle before all your changes and new projects can fully take shape.

Don, the president of an IT company, stretched his wings the year he turned fifty, a 1 Personal Year. In typical 13/4 Life Path fashion, he had dedicated the better part of his years to family and career. A few years before, he had purchased a motorcycle, which he enjoyed riding to and from the office and other short distances. True to his cautious, reliable, and dependable 4 Life Path, Don had never been much of a risk taker. That year, with the children grown up and the company well established, he felt confident enough to venture out into the world. He joined a local motorcycle club and signed on for a 2,200-mile, ten-day ride to the East Coast. This was a challenging trek for a novice rider, but fuelled by his fresh new 1 Personal Year energy, he was ready.

Note that when you reach a Personal Year that has the same numerical value as your Life Path number, this can be a very significant time of life. It is as though your Life Path number becomes supercharged, and its energy needs to manifest itself in an urgent manner. If you have not mastered this number, or are expressing negative aspects of it, these negative traits may be exaggerated at this time. Additional self-awareness is helpful during these intense periods. In Natalie's case, her 19/1 Life Path energy becomes highly activated in a 1 Personal Year. At the time she entered college, at the end of a 9 Personal Year, she also began a new relationship. Barely a couple of days into the following 1 Personal Year, a 2 Personal Month, to her chagrin, she ended the relationship. The intensity of the 1 energy did not lend itself well to resolving relationship issues at that time of her life, and so not surprisingly, she chose to forge ahead on her own.

In a 1 Personal Year, keep in mind that you are at the beginning of a new cycle. It can take up to two years before the energy of change is fully manifested and takes its place in your life. Do not expect results to happen right away; you have the next several years to develop your projects. You may need to exercise a little patience, especially if you have quick-minded and quick-acting numbers like the 1 and the 5 among your core numbers.

CHAPTER 4 • THE 1 PERSONAL YEAR

The 1 Personal Year Month by Month

JANUARY (2 Personal Month): New Beginnings, Receptivity

On the heels of a 9 Personal Year, the 1 Personal Year can be an exciting time, with new perspectives and a renewed sense of vigour and energy. You may still be reeling from the emotional intensity and fatigue of your recently ended epicycle, but expectations for the future are starting to grow. You may need to deal with relationship issues as you embark on a new long-term cycle. Use diplomacy and tact in dealing with others. Study any new plans or ideas that came up at the end of last year. Take the time to allow things to fall into place. There is no need to rush now. Clear up any loose ends remaining from last year. Pay attention to feedback from the universe around you. If you are experiencing any doubts about your new direction, examine their origins for validity. Change can cause fear and uncertainty, and a 1 Personal Year is often a year of big changes.

FEBRUARY (3 Personal Month): Creative Expression, Optimism

You are probably going to be feeling much more optimistic this month; in fact, you're ready to take on the world! Your creative energies are beginning to flow as you start to realize that a new cycle has effectively begun. Imagination, which may have lain dormant for some time now, is reawakened and new ideas start to rise to the surface. You express yourself well now, and are open to new opportunities. You feel lucky and hopeful, and you are ready to embark on your new life direction. Take advantage of your social contacts as you begin to leave the past behind and start on your new journey. Explore your options, but take the time to think things through. Enjoy some fun activities.

MARCH (4 Personal Month): Organization, Work, Order

Now is the time to buckle down and concentrate on your new projects and goals. This is a foundation month, and your ability to work hard and pay attention to details will determine whether or not your projects will get off to a strong start. You may need to get yourself focused and organized, especially if last month you allowed yourself to become distracted or overly scattered. Begin to build a practical and effective plan for your goals. If you are well organized, you will feel less restricted as you get down to work. You are very productive now and much can be accomplished. You may need to give up some of your social time to pull this off. Fear not, growth follows shortly. Don't ignore those home projects; make time for family.

APRIL (5 Personal Month): Adventure, The Unexpected

If you have started off with a solid foundation, the new opportunities presented this month will contribute nicely to the growth and expansion of your projects. Travel is possible. Unusual or unique opportunities may arise. This is a time of experimentation, adventure, and excitement. Approach new opportunities with an open mind, but keep one foot on the ground. This is a good time for personal, career, and business growth. Apply some of those new ideas and approaches that have been stirring, as you will encounter opportunities for them to be expressed. Stick to your plan if you don't want to veer off course. Leave some free time in your schedule; you will need a little freedom this month.

MAY (6 Personal Month): Balance, Responsibility

If you are involved in a service-related industry, changes and new approaches may be tried out now. Tend to responsibilities. You will need to maintain balance between your work and personal life, keeping loved ones informed of your new direction, projects, and ideas. Others may feel insecure as you proceed with new plans this year. Let family and friends know that you will not be leaving them behind. If there are unexpressed issues in your personal relationships, try to bring them out with sensitivity and compassion. In all matters, remain true to your values.

JUNE (7 Personal Month): Reflection, Analysis, Study

Career moves to the back burner as you pause to think things through. Are your goals clear at this time? Review your planning and goal-setting for the year and make adjustments as necessary. Take some quiet time out, meditate, practice yoga, or read a book. Also, do any background work, study, or research, that may help ensure the accomplishment of your goals. This is a time of learning, understanding, depth, and insight. Yet, try to keep a balance between your inner focus and your personal relationships. Avoid selfishly excluding loved ones. Instead, simply let them know that you need a little quiet time.

JULY (8 Personal Month): Plans, Career, Focus

July is a power month in a year of new beginnings. This is a great time to get your projects moving forward or to expand your career or business activities. You should start to experience some progress now as the energy of your new epicycle becomes fully engaged. Your focus this month should be on career and finances. This can be a profitable month as business and financial activities take on more importance. You are in a good position to reap the rewards of the efforts of the past few months. Important new professional relationships may be started now. If you must take your vacation this month, you might find it difficult to take your mind off work. If you can, schedule your vacation for next month, or November.

AUGUST (9 Personal Month): Release, Completion

You will find it easy to bring some of your plans to completion this month. Whatever was holding you back can be easily released now. Be willing to let go of restrictions, old habits, outdated relationships, and behaviours. Free yourself of any remaining obstacles and blockages that may hinder your progress, any issues that remain from last year, a 9 Personal Year. You may also choose to let go of some of the least appropriate new ideas you came up with this year. Focus on a positive attitude, and avoid being consumed by fear or feelings of loss. Look forward, not backward. Your new cycle will be completely set in motion next month. Leave your comfort zone, go out, extend, and stretch yourself. Volunteer in your community; do something for others. Treat yourself to a nice leisurely vacation.

SEPTEMBER (1 Personal Month): Action, Initiative

A 1 Month in a 1 Year! Expect much movement and energy this month. Be ready to step it up and manifest! Be bold, be daring. Express your uniqueness, your creativity, and your leadership ability. Leave all your fears behind. Begin a new lifestyle, plan a new business or passion project, start a health regimen, or join a gym. This is your chance to steer your life in a new direction, where you can really make important changes, or if necessary, a fresh new start. A new relationship could be burgeoning; next month you will know whether or not you wish to pursue it. Make sure the actions you undertake reflect your current long-term direction and goals. Focus on yourself, your needs, and your desires without being overly selfish. Avoid alienating others. Begin to take those important steps that will lead you substantially closer to your goals.

OCTOBER (2 Personal Month): Patience, Receptivity

You'll need to be patient as the pace slows down a bit this month. The new projects you started will take time to develop and take shape. Pay attention to details. Keep an open mind, and be receptive to external feedback as well as to inner guidance. Others may provide valuable input, contributing in a positive way to the growth of your ideas and projects. Cooperation could be of benefit. You are more sensitive and intuitive than usual and may take things to heart. A new romance could bloom now. If you have a partner, light up the romance in your relationship. Take the time to catch your breath and re-establish a sense of peace and harmony. Reconnect with those who are close to you. You are not alone. Your next Personal Year, a 2, will bring relationships to the fore.

NOVEMBER (3 Personal Month): Enthusiasm, Joie de Vivre, Creativity

New projects are well underway by now, so you can relax a little and enjoy life. A positive, enthusiastic attitude will move you forward and inspire others to join with you. You feel as though you are on top of the world and your optimism is contagious. Be careful not to become too distracted or to scatter your energies. With an endless stream of new ideas rising to the surface, you may find it difficult to focus on your goals and your work. It is more difficult to remain disciplined this month; there are just too many fun things to do, too many social events, dinner parties, and other distractions. Do take the time to enjoy the company of friends while maintaining a focus on your goals. And stick to your budget!

DECEMBER (4 Personal Month): Work, Work, Work.

Like March, December is a time to re-establish structure and organization in your life, but now that your new cycle is well established, you will want to focus your energies on strengthening your foundation. Last month's burst of creativity and great ideas can now be put to good use. You will need to pay attention to details, order, and routine. Home and family may also require your attention. If you get yourself organized, things will go more smoothly. Although progress will at times appear to be slow, your efforts and dedication will pay off in the long run. Hang in there. Check your work habits and day-to-day routine for efficiency; eliminate time wasters.

Exercise 1: Preparing for Your 1 Personal Year

1. Relative to your Life Path, Birth Day number, and personal experience of the number 1, how do you feel about new beginnings? Do you have difficulty being autonomous and taking initiative? Are you comfortable starting new projects? If you are lacking in autonomy and confidence, look for support from a coach or friend while you attempt to make changes in your life.

2. Recall the last time you experienced a 1 Personal Year. (See the "My Personal History" exercise in Chapter 3.) What new activities did you begin? What significant changes did you make at the time? If everything remained the same as in previous years, that is, if you did not make any changes, was it because your life was right on track, or because you were fearful of change? Over the years that followed your last 1 Personal Year, did you reach your goals?

3. Relative to where you are now, what new element(s) do you need to integrate into your life? For example, if you have an 8 Life Path and haven't yet manifested your full power potential, this would be a good time to take a first step. What one activity could you do that would help you integrate your personal power? If you have a 2 Life Path and haven't yet overcome your co-dependency issues, what one thing could you do to improve or heal this situation? What activity could you undertake that would help you develop self-reliance? Now would be a good time to begin that special project or activity that has for too long been relegated to the "one day when…" pile.

4. Review your Key Life Sectors list. (See "Exercise: Key Life Sectors" in Chapter 3.) Are all these sectors relevant in your life at this time? Remove old sectors, and add new ones based on the new direction you are choosing for yourself now.

5. Find one new activity or goal to be accomplished this year for each of your Key Life Sectors. Bringing new elements into your life will invigorate you in many ways. Set new goals for each sector. For example, you may want to reach a new level in your job, or attain a new health benchmark. Set specific, measurable goals. Create a plan for the achievement of these goals. March and December of the 1 Personal Year—4 Personal Months—are excellent months to work on your plans. Be realistic in determining your objectives for the year. Setting unrealistic expectations or goals is more likely to lead to failure.

6. Toxic relationships are as harmful as bad habits. Move away from harmful or outdated relationships. People will not always agree with your new ideas and plans, and may not be supportive as you move forward with your life.

Exercise 2: Year-End Review

1. What new directions did your life take this year? In what areas did you express increased initiative, self-reliance, and courage?

2. What are the benefits of these changes?

3. What is the most important lesson you learned this year?

4. What new knowledge will you bring into your upcoming 2 Personal Year?

CHAPTER 5

The 2 Personal Year

Cooperation, Receptivity, Adaptability

The dynamic and expressive energy of the 1 projects itself outward until the 1 becomes 2. This establishes a state of duality: myself and others, action and response, inner and outer, dynamic and static. That which manifested from the core of the self in the 1 Personal Year, must now find its proper place and form outside itself. Having become 2, the 1 is now polarized. This can create tension, both within and without. Whereas in the last year there was a sense of limitless possibilities, now boundaries, obstacles, and limitations are beginning to appear.

It is not uncommon to experience feelings of frustration and impatience in a 2 Personal Year. This is a time for cooperation and receptivity. Yet, as much as you need to be cooperative at this stage of your development, you may be overly sensitive to the input of others, even resentful of the meddling and intrusion of outside forces. The new projects and activities you began last year are still vulnerable in their early stages of development.

You realize now that you are not alone. You can either do battle against perceived external obstacles, or learn to work with them. You may benefit by taking advantage of the resources available outside yourself. Depending on your ability to cooperate and work with others, you will either thrive with the help and support of others, or suffer the frustration of having to share, to be open to the ideas of others and make compromises. If you have a 1, 5, or 8 Life Path, you may experience some impatience with the need to wait for the input of others to move forward with your projects.

While the 2 Personal Year may bring you face-to-face with the responses from the world outside yourself, it will also bring out your inner reactions to the initiatives that you undertook in your 1 Personal Year. This is where you may encounter insecurities, fears, or doubts about your newly formed projects or ideas. If you are prone to doubting and second-guessing yourself, you may have to struggle hard at this time to maintain sufficient focus on your goals.

If this is an 11/2 Year, your antennas will likely be fully charged. The universe may show you alternate routes or different ways of approaching your new projects. By maintaining an open mind and being receptive to your environment, you can gain valuable insights about your direction and purpose. With this additional information, you can make the necessary changes and adjustments that will allow you to be more successful in the long term.

This is a time of increased interaction with others, not just personal, but also social, business, and professional. You may be dealing with perceptions that will need to be reconciled, viewpoints that must be discussed, and future plans that will require adjustments, cooperation, and fine-tuning. This is a great healing time for relationships. A budding romantic relationship may be ready to be taken to the next step. The 2 Year is a very common time for marriage.

Be patient, observant, and receptive; you will be better prepared. Choose a course of action that reflects your inner desires, rather than one designed to accommodate your fears or insecurities. If you are a people-pleaser, beware of doing things just to make someone else happy, while ignoring your own goals in the process. Take your time when making decisions. If necessary, seek guidance or counselling; get help to deal with challenges or blockages. Take the time to meditate, study, plan, and assimilate the energies at work in your life. Your 9-Year Epicycle is young

CHAPTER 5 · THE 2 PERSONAL YEAR

and just beginning to take shape. Take the time you need to establish yourself firmly.

The 2 Personal Year brings out all forms of interaction with others, and often requires that you be flexible, cooperative, and adaptable, and that you make adjustments as necessary. It favours contacts, associations, and relationships with women in particular. It is important to think of others, not only of yourself during this time. As this is a relational year during which you are probably adjusting to new directions, remember to be mindful of the impact of your actions on loved ones. Be tactful and sensitive. This can be a period of stress in your encounters with others, especially if difficulties and unexpressed grievances have been building up. Good communication skills, patience, and understanding will help you reconcile your differences.

The 2 Personal Year is an excellent time to seek professional help such as counselling, coaching, therapy, or mentoring. Positive, constructive support at this early and often delicate time of the new epicycle can be very productive. At the same time, it is important to be discerning in your choice of confidants. In the early stages of your epicycle, you may be vulnerable to the negative opinions of others. A cynical comment can quickly take the wind out of your sails and stop you in your progress.

Robert, an accountant with a history of failed relationships and too many career changes, decided to take matters in hand. In his 2 Personal Year, with a 13/4 Life Path, he undertook a process with a therapist to uncover the reasons for the failure of his relationships. He also hired a personal coach to help him define a clear career path. These steps gave him the tools and the confidence he needed to approach these important aspects of his life in a healthy manner. He admitted that this is not something that he would normally have done, but it seemed fitting at that particular time of his life. The counselling and the coaching gave him the clarity and direction he needed to set him on track.

Phase II Thinking

We are all familiar with the exhilarating energy of the number 1. It begins with a great idea. Excitedly, you discuss it with a close friend. Anything is possible in this initial phase; no obstacle is so great that it couldn't possibly be dealt with. You suddenly feel clever, inspired, and invigorated as new life flows through your veins. You experience joy and confidence; nothing can stop you. Your entire existence has new meaning. You begin to plan and speculate; you imagine what it will be like and how you will feel once you have achieved your brand-new goal.

What almost inevitably follows this exciting new beginning is the reaction phase. The 2 is defined as the number of receptivity, emotional response, and sensitivity to others and to environmental factors. While the 1 represents all that is pure yang (pure male energy), the 2 is pure yin (pure female energy), geared toward survival rather than toward adventure. The 2 is emotional and intuitive rather than rational; it is reactive and receptive rather than proactive and dynamic. Even if it isn't one of your core numbers, you will regularly experience the energy of the number 2, because it naturally follows the 1. Whenever you experience a beginning, you will experience a reaction, or a response.

Typically, the day following the manifestation of your brilliant new idea, you will encounter the reaction phase, or the doubting phase. This is where you face the inner dialogue, often manifesting as various forms of resistance: *I couldn't possibly do that... What a dumb idea... What was I thinking? It's too much work... I don't have what it takes... It would take too long... I don't have the time... I don't have the money... My partner would never go for it...* I call it the Backtalk. Suddenly, the list of reasons for not following through with your new idea grows longer than the list of reasons why you should pursue it. The initial enthusiasm begins to wane. Discouragement, fear, and disappointment drown out passion and optimism. Exhilaration quickly fades, and the next

CHAPTER 5 • THE 2 PERSONAL YEAR

thing you know, another great idea is abandoned and returned to the realm of the formless, unrealized potential.

Recognize the pattern? I call it Phase II Thinking, the reaction. This is a hurdle many people encounter when undergoing a process of personal growth and transformation. Most people have experienced it, to greater or lesser degrees, at least a few times in their lives. However, each time you succumb to the negative dialogue of the 2 energy, you reinforce a pattern of failure, leaving behind a trail of faltering hopes and missed opportunities. Sometimes, it is better to make an honest attempt and fail, rather than not make any attempt at all. Very often, it is in the learning obtained while attempting something, even if it leads to failure, that we gain the knowledge or the keys required for reaching subsequent successes.

The 2 Personal Year needn't automatically lead to dead ends, or prevent you from fulfilling your dreams. The key to managing Phase II Thinking is to not allow yourself to remain locked in its negative processes. A certain amount of caution, reflection, and analysis is good. But first take your idea, study it in terms of desirability and feasibility, then look at the obstacles as well as the potential benefits of finding solutions and pursuing its full development. Phase II is natural and even necessary. It calls on discernment. If you didn't take the time to go through it, you would constantly be throwing yourself in the direction of any and every idea that came your way, and in the end, little would be accomplished.

Relinquishing Family Grievances

A 2 Year is often a time for love and romance. If you began a new relationship last year, it may grow to the next level this year. Marriage is common in a 2 Personal Year. Feeling more emotional and vulnerable than normal, you may seek the support, affection, and protection of someone close. There is a need to share. The following is adapted from an article published in my online newsletter many years ago. It sums up my experience of a very important number 2 Personal Year and is included here as inspiration for those who might be looking for an enjoyable way to deepen their relationships or reconnect with family members.

In the fall of 2005, the Sun conjoined Jupiter in the sign of Libra, a cardinal air sign, ruled by Venus, the planet of love, values, and relationships. It is the sign of social interaction, marriage, and partnerships of all kinds. Libras love to talk, discuss, debate, and chat on a variety of topics, in various environments. Rare is the Libra who has nothing to say on a subject, no matter how shy or reclusive they may be.

My dad, with his Libra Moon, was no exception. He loved family gatherings: Christmas, Easter, and grandchildren's birthdays—he was there. As a Taurus, also a Venus-ruled sign, he was quite the gourmet, or I should say more precisely, *gourmand!* On October 17th, the day of the lunar eclipse, it would have been six months since my father passed away. Much had happened in our lives since then. It was a period of adjustment for all of us—parents, children, and grandchildren alike—as we scrambled to fill the gap left behind by his unexpected departure. Without a plan or script to follow, we somehow managed to pull together, being there for each other whenever the need arose, no questions asked. Pulling together was the natural thing to do.

In my consultation work, and also socially, I often heard people complain about their families: parents, in-laws, children, siblings... the list of complaints was long and often quite colourful. Family ties are easily taken for granted in a time when a family can be easily destroyed simply by being in the wrong place on the planet at the wrong time. In our family, May had always been a month of celebrations, with the birthdays of my daughters, my nephew, and my dad. And then there was Mother's day, Victoria Day, and Father's Day in June—plenty of opportunities for dinners and the first barbecues of summer. For us, the dinner schedule for that first summer without my dad was conspicuously meagre.

CHAPTER 5 · THE 2 PERSONAL YEAR

Alone now, with my daughters living far across town, I decided to institute Sunday family dinners, something I had wanted to do for years. Cooking and experimenting with cuisines from around the world was a pleasure I shared with my daughters, and when Caroline mentioned that she missed my home cooking, it didn't take much for me to set my plan in motion. I'd been craving a good homemade Moroccan couscous. Couscous was way too much food for one, even two people. So this would be my first dinner. I let the word out that I would be making a couscous on the first Sunday of August. Cook it and they will come, I thought cleverly. In that moment, Family, Friends, and Food was born.

And they came! My daughters and their friends and my mom and one of my brothers. We had a lovely time and a real hoot playing a dictionary game. This was our first gathering since my dad's passing. The following month, four more members added themselves to our family dinner, including my other brother and his wife. Together we enjoyed a night of sushi and sake. Although the dinners toggled between Saturdays and Sundays, adjusting to suit everyone's schedules (a wonderful number 2 trait), they became a monthly event for our family. Everyone participated, enthusiastically searching the Internet and cookbooks for unique recipe ideas and cultural tidbits and anecdotes. We feasted on a variety of cuisines from around the world, with theme menus planned months in advance, including country French cuisine, Nova Scotia seafood, Szechwan, traditional Greek fare, the cuisine of Brazil, Thailand, California, Mexico, down-home Quebec, and a Passover Seder thrown in for good measure.

A true gastronome, my dad would have loved those gatherings. When we came together for dinner, I felt as though he was right there, watching over us, smiling, pleased that we had moved on, relieved that we had taken care of each other and that my mom was okay and we were looking out for each other. In a way, those dinners were a tribute to his memory. What a wonderful 2 Personal Year experience!

The next time you feel yourself projecting a grievance toward a family member, perhaps you might want to consider the impermanence of the world in which we live. And in that moment between thought and action, that special instant in which you are free to choose, you might consider relinquishing your grievance and choosing love instead. Holding a grievance will not make you feel any better, but choosing love absolutely will.

The 2 Personal Year Month by Month

Note that if you are using the Master number 11 in your calculations for the Personal Year, the Personal Month numbers will be slightly different, either expressing as High Energy numbers, or Master numbers. February, for example would be a 13/4 month (11 + 2 = 13). This would apply also to March, May, August, and December. November would be a 22/4 month (11 + 11 = 22), rather than a 13/4.

JANUARY (3 Personal Month): Social Life, Creativity, Communication

What a great way to start the new year! The energy and optimism of the number 3 is always welcome. Although social contacts are emphasized now, keep in mind that as this is a 2 Personal Year, you would do well to keep some of your new ideas and plans to yourself. You are still in a process of inner change and growth, and may be vulnerable to the influence of others. Be discriminating in your choice of confidants. What you need now, above all else, is the support of a positive ally. Surround yourself with optimistic and success-minded individuals. This can be a romantic time; if single, you could meet someone who strikes your fancy; if you are in a relationship, spice it up a little, take some time out to enjoy your partner's company. Don't be shy; express your creativity!

CHAPTER 5 • THE 2 PERSONAL YEAR

FEBRUARY (4 Personal Month): Work, Focus, Cooperation

As with all 4 Personal Months, you will need to focus on details and work this month. You may want to spend time on a home renovation project with your spouse, or family member, especially a project that helps promote order and organization. Your dedication and earnestness are inspiring, but remember to remain sensitive to other people's ideas as you dive into the tasks at hand. Although you are keen on getting the job done, be cooperative, diplomatic, and delicate. Things may not be moving as rapidly as you would like, given your thrust of new number 1 energy from the previous year. Learning to work in harmony with others is part of the lesson in a 2 Personal Year. Attend to money and financial matters this month.

MARCH (5 Personal Month): Opportunities, Travel, Surprises

You will need to be extra flexible this month, as unexpected circumstances may come into play. Avoid risky ventures and stay away from get-rich-quick schemes. If it looks too good to be true, it probably is. This could be an adventurous and exciting month. Use innovative approaches to express yourself or to market your services. Try to do things a little differently. Opportunities may present themselves as you meet new people. Think twice before turning your back on a relationship that appears to have grown old with time. Remain rational and don't lose your focus. Be sincere in your interactions with others; skip the idle flirtations. Do something fun, different, and exciting with your partner. A 2 Personal Year is one of slow growth.

APRIL (6 Personal Month): Balance, Family, Service

You may have the opportunity to reconnect with an old acquaintance, or a relationship that has served its time could be re-evaluated or even come to an end. Friends, coworkers, or family members may need your help more than usual this month. Responsibilities at work are also on the rise, and your ability to deal with situations in a harmonious and peaceful manner will leave you in good stead with your employers and coworkers. Use diplomacy and sensitivity in delicate or difficult situations. Arrange a romantic getaway with your partner. You need balance to be productive; review your weekly calendar and make sure you haven't been led off course. Your people skills will either be tested or put to good use.

MAY (7 Personal Month): Reflection, Intuition, Reserve

Plan for some quiet, peaceful time by yourself, even if it's just to sort through an old book or music collection, or find a solution for a long-standing problem. Study, do some research, explore a deeper aspect of yourself, your work, or your craft. You may want to examine the new plans you made last year and make any adjustments, based on what you have learned to date this year. Remember, a 2 Personal Year is a time to be receptive. Study the messages you've been given; look for guidance. Don't force yourself to produce visible results now. Be sensitive to close ones while you become introspective. Let them know you need a little time by yourself; reassure them that you are not pulling away on a permanent basis. This is not a good month for planning big social events.

JUNE (8 Personal Month): Power, Negotiation, Accomplishment

The relationships you have cultivated so far this year are starting to bear fruit. This is a time of much activity and progress in joint projects. Maintain an unhurried pace in all endeavours. Your plans are starting to take shape, and you are probably feeling much more confident and self-empowered than you have over the past couple of months. Use your power to negotiate a gain, but do so in a diplomatic way. Career advancement is possible now.

CHAPTER 5 • THE 2 PERSONAL YEAR

This is a good time to handle financial affairs. Avoid becoming drawn into a power struggle. Look for harmonious solutions in all situations. Your focus is on career, and business contacts and interactions this month.

JULY (9 Personal Month): Completion, Release, Endings

Even though you are feeling that progress has been a bit slow this year, finishing off certain aspects of your projects this month will give you a sense of accomplishment. A special relationship may come to an end. This can be an emotional time, as you let go of outdated ties, habits, or activities. You could be experiencing moments of doubt and uncertainty. Pursue an activity that revolves around helping others; give a little of yourself. This will help deflate any pent-up emotions you may be feeling as a result of releasing the past. Spend time outdoors, or just take some time off. This is a month of endings; new beginnings will come in the next month. Allow things to come to a close naturally, without resistance, blame, or criticism. Any unsettled feelings will resolve themselves next month. Focus on your accomplishments rather than on the past.

AUGUST (1 Personal Month): Renewed Energy, Cooperative Ventures

Joint projects or cooperative ventures take on new energy and direction now. You are feeling reborn, and ready to more forward now. But you are still in the early stages of your new epicycle. Time is required to allow your ideas and projects to develop and reach maturity. Impatience will only set you back and cause you frustration. Although you may be eager to move forward with your plans, remember that this is a 2 Personal Year, and as such, it requires that you wait while conditions mature and are made ready. Also, you may need the support of others to develop your projects, so keep those lines of communication open. Avoid impulsive moves. Maintain a steady pace. An opportunity may arise where you can use your leadership skills. Give of yourself generously. Others will benefit from your experience.

SEPTEMBER (11/2 Personal Month): Intuition, Sensitivity, Idealism

This could be an intense month, with increased opportunities for interacting with others. You may experience some self-doubt now, especially if you have shared your plans with people who are not supportive of your ideas. You are particularly sensitive to the opinions of others. If possible, stay away from negative people. With the heightened sensitivity of the Master number 11, you could feel inspired from deep within. Your intuition is highly tuned, and you may be guided by your inner voice, or through dreams. Keep your feet on the ground and stay focused on your goals. Avoid reaching for more than you can handle. Above all, be tactful and diplomatic this month. Note that if this is an 11/2 Personal Year, September will be a Basic number 2 Month (11 + 9 = 20; 2 + 0 = 2). This may be a relief, as your antennas have been supercharged all year.

OCTOBER (3 Personal Month): Pleasure, Creativity, Relaxation

Following the intensity of last month, you are probably ready for a little fun time out now. Plan a vacation or some enjoyable outings or activities with friends. Continue to be patient and to pace your efforts. Progress will come in due time. You are more playful, positive, and optimistic now, and your creativity is heightened. Try to express this creative energy in your work, or in your relationships. Take some time out for the arts, go to a movie, a stand-up comedy show, the theatre, or dust off your guitar and pick and make some music of your own. You could enjoy a romantic tête-à-tête. Avoid overly stressful situations this month. Remember to stay on track, as much as possible.

CHAPTER 5 • THE 2 PERSONAL YEAR

NOVEMBER (13/4 Personal Month): Hard Work, Focus, Practicality

Hopefully you managed to take some fun time off last month, because now you'll need to get organized and focus on the tasks at hand. You could be feeling unfairly pressed to take care of details, or overwhelmed by the amount of work that is piling up on your desk. The most effective approach will be to simply get down to business. The more you resist and fight it, the more restricted you will feel. Before complaining about your burdens, keep in mind that this is a stabilizing month, and dealing with commitments and foundation issues will give you the strength, courage, and security to move forward with your plans next year. Put your nose to the grindstone and you will see results.

DECEMBER (5 Personal Month): Change, Surprises, Freedom

As much as last month forced you to deal with the details of your work, this month brings change and surprises. Be flexible. This is a good month for standing up and allowing yourself to shine. Try new and unusual approaches. Don't walk the beaten path; be innovative. Flexibility and open-mindedness will be an asset. You do need a bit of freedom and fun, so try to unload, or temporarily set aside, some of your excess responsibilities. Review your list of priorities and deal with the really important matters first. Save the menial tasks for later. Travel and new experiences are possible this month. It could be difficult for you to focus on responsibilities at this time.

Exercise 1: Preparing for Your 2 Personal Year

1. Relative to your Life Path, Birth Day number, and personal experience of the number 2, how are you faring in your relationships, both personal and professional? Do you have difficulty relating to others or being attentive to the needs of those who are close to you? How do you feel about being

receptive in general? Are you a go-getter, always in charge? If so, how do you get feedback from your environment if you are not receptive?

2. Go back to the last time you experienced a 2 Personal Year. (See the "My Personal History" exercise in Chapter 3.) What was going on in your relationships at that time? How did you deal with your emotional responses to the circumstances of your life? Did you experience peace and harmony in your personal relationships? If not, why not? How did you react to new projects begun the previous year? Were you successful in overcoming any Phase II objections?

3. Relative to where you are in your life at this time, how would you like to see your relationships improve? For example, if you are a freedom-loving 5 Life Path person with a trail of broken relationships behind you, what might you do to bring stability into your relationships? If you are a deep-thinking 7 Life Path, consider how your solitary, introspective nature has affected your ability to build strong personal relationships. If you are a strong 8 type, usually caught up in career matters, how can you bring more balance into your life?

4. Review your Key Life Sectors list. Are all these sectors relevant in your life at this time? Have you set aside time for special relationships? If not, make any necessary changes or adjustments.

5. Take the time to heal relationship issues. Work on developing new business and professional relationships. Deepen old business and professional relationships. Get in touch with coworkers, clients or customers. Learn more about their needs. Take special time out for family. Update your relationships with your children. Their needs grow as they do. Give a little extra time to aging parents. They won't be around forever. Don't ignore those pesky customers. They may have something of value to convey to you. Pay attention

to difficult relationships; they will teach you much about yourself.

6. Do you have any negative, Phase II types of responses or objections to your fresh new start of last year? If your objections stem from a negative attitude, such as fear of failure, self-criticism, excessive perfectionism, or lack of self-confidence, what can you do to change these unhealthy habits? Affirmations and creative visualization are examples of effective tools for dealing with these types of behaviour.

7. Would it be beneficial for you to develop a relationship with a mentor or coach? This would be a good time to join a peer advisory group. If there isn't one in your area, start one.

8. If you are taking a personal relationship to the next level, such as marriage, have you openly discussed your hopes, plans, and expectations for the future? Get things out in the open before you embark on a lifelong journey together. Explore your true motives for making this decision at this time. In this progressive age, surprisingly, still too many people marry for the wrong reasons.

Exercise 2: Year-End Review

1. In what ways did you improve your relationships this year? What have you learned about being receptive and open to outside help?

2. What are the benefits of these changes?

3. What is the most important lesson you learned this year?

4. What new knowledge will you bring into your upcoming 3 Personal Year?

CHAPTER 6

The 3 Personal Year

Creativity, Self-Expression, Joie de Vivre

When you move into a 3 Personal Year, it is not unusual to experience a feeling of relief, like a valve opening up releasing pent-up steam. The joining of one with another, the 2 experienced last year, now produces a third energy, just as the fusion of sperm and egg produces an embryo. The energy of the 3 Personal Year helps relieve much of the tension caused by the polarization of forces that may have been experienced in the previous 2 Personal Year. Last year the focus was on balancing all aspects of relationships. It was self and other; seeing that my needs are met while yours are being met.

In the 3 Year, energy explodes, possibilities abound, and what seemed previously guarded and tentative, too sensitive to be brought forth, too vulnerable to be exposed to external scrutiny and potential criticism, now begins to bubble to the surface. New projects and ideas that emerged over the past two years are now seeking an outlet for uninhibited manifestation. What was on your mind is ready to be expressed.

During the 3 Personal Year, you will find the pace of activity stepping up considerably. Last year, in your 2 Personal Year, you may have encountered delays, objections, or reactions—some internal, some external, some expected, others not—to your previous 1 Personal Year initiatives. You may have felt that things were not moving as quickly as you would have liked. Forget the past, that trend will change this year. The expanding energy of the number 3 will offer you multiple opportunities to be social, have more fun, and express yourself in whatever way you enjoy, whether through writing, blogging, painting, speaking, theatre, crafts, socializing, or good old-fashioned dinner parties. You will generally have more personal freedom to do all those things that you are eager to accomplish. Doors open more easily in a 3 Personal Year. People make things happen for you, and income can increase. This is an excellent year to broaden your relationship spheres and to expand your personal and business network of contacts. You express yourself well now, and can get your ideas across with creative flair and originality. But one important tip: make a budget! All those activities can cost a few pennies.

Michel, a 22/4 Life Path with an 11/2 Birth Day, is a highly gifted musician and composer. In a 3 Personal Year, he was invited to participate with two other composers in the production and recording of their cello sonatas for a promotional CD. This welcome opportunity was also accompanied by a public concert. All this came about through knowing the right people in the right places. It isn't uncommon for people to catch lucky breaks in a 3 energy. Interestingly, Michel's cello sonata had initially been composed in the 1 Personal Year of the previous epicycle. Often, projects begun in a 1 Personal Year are not brought to completion right away; by the same token, it does not necessarily follow that everything you begin in a 1 Year will become a great accomplishment.

This book was produced in a burst of creative energy during a 3 Personal Year, a record for me, since it had previously taken me twenty years to complete two other works. Additionally, in that same year, I set up the structure for three other writing projects. If you have a creative side, you may find that the 3 Year can be a very fertile period.

The 3 Personal Year has the potential for being a really fun year, as it favours shared pleasures, personal expression, social expansion, lucky breaks, creativity, affection, relationships, romance, and simply enjoying life. To avoid waste and dispersion

CHAPTER 6 · THE 3 PERSONAL YEAR

of your energies and resources, you will have to work at keeping things focused. Moderation is key now. Avoid hasty decision making; remember to think things through and to apply restraint. In a 3 Personal Year there can be a tendency of being extravagant, perhaps even overly optimistic, especially if you have many 3s among your core numbers.

With opportunities on the rise, it's easy to become scattered. You could find yourself taking on far too many projects. In the end, you'll be disappointed since you'll have to abandon the extra activities, even though they seemed like a good idea at the time. Just because something looks good doesn't mean that you should take it on. It's important to keep an eye on your long-term goals now. But focusing on your goals doesn't have to feel like a chore, or a restricting obligation. Use your creativity to stay on track.

An excellent and fun tool for helping you stay focused is to make a collage that depicts your goals. Find images that represent these goals. Pin them to your wall or on a bulletin board next to your work area. You can also set up a binder with a section for each of your Key Life Sectors. As goals are reached, you can remove the pages; then add new ones as new goals emerge. It may sound a little grade-schoolish, but, besides being lots of fun, having clear pictures can help you stay on track. What's more, who said that planning and goal setting couldn't be fun?

For some people, creativity is a tender commodity, to be treated delicately and with great nurturing. In a world that generally favours conventions over originality, it can be difficult to break through the confines of conformity and dare to express ideas that go against the common currents. You may have to handle your creative ideas with care. Avoid discussing your fledgling ideas with people who may not be in line with your thinking. For some reason, it seems that it is easier for many people to find fault in something new than it is to see its qualities or potential value. If your best friend is habitually negative and critical, don't discuss your new idea with them. Instead, find someone you trust, someone who has a positive attitude, and someone who will be supportive rather than destructive. Most people have enough self-destructive ammunition within themselves as it is. You certainly don't need to leave home to find more!

If you wish to prevent the destruction of your dreams and give them a fighting chance against Phase II Thinking, consciously channel energy into your creative thinking process this year. If you haven't dealt with your Phase II Thinking, you might find yourself being overly critical of any fresh, new ideas. Decide now to have a positive attitude toward yourself and your projects.

If you habitually maintain negative thinking habits, now would be an excellent time for an attitude adjustment. Practise saying *yes* instead of *no*. In a 3 Personal Year, typically you will have plenty of opportunities to practise saying yes, as you are more socially inclined and more optimistic than usual. In a 3 Year, people are inclined to approach you more readily for a variety of requests and opportunities. You may receive invitations to participate in fundraising, social, or business events. Don't worry, once you've reached your quota and your calendar is full, you can learn to politely say no. Simply explain that you are fully booked but would love to help out next time.

Elizabeth, a financial security advisor with a 22/4 Life Path, came up with what she felt was a fabulous idea to promote her business. She visualized herself hosting a wine-and-cheese and art appreciation fundraiser in a gallery for her clients and friends. She saw this as a way of promoting the friendlier side of herself while deepening relationships with the people who could drive business her way, an excellent business approach for a highly competitive field. We had already discussed the creative possibilities available to her, given that she was now in a 3 Personal Year. She sounded very excited as she described her plan to me over the phone, but as she approached the end of her story, I could hear the "yeah buts" pushing to the surface, ready to cast dark shadows on her bright new idea. And then the Phase II Thinking kicked in.

CHAPTER 6 · THE 3 PERSONAL YEAR

When we took a closer look at her perceived objections, she quickly came to realize that they were symbolic of her old way of negative thinking. In fact, she soon discovered that there was no real foundation for her objections. At this point, she reaffirmed her intention to adjust her attitude and proceeded to work on the action plan that would ensure the success of her new marketing venture. As it turned out, the event was a great success, and raised far more money than she had initially anticipated.

Over the course of many years, Linda, a 3 Life Path with a 3 Birthday, explored a variety of career options, including aesthetics, therapeutic massage, modeling, and style and image consulting. Her positive attitude and friendly disposition allowed her to pursue each of these avenues with a certain degree of success, though she felt that she was very scattered throughout most of her life. Until her mid-forties, she had not quite fully tapped into her truly creative and artistic side. In a 3 Personal Year, Linda's creativity found a perfect outlet. Now in a happy and loving relationship, she was able to return to one of her early passions, the world of watercolour. She took lessons and started to experiment with a variety of materials, until in a matter of a few years, she became fully engaged as a painter. Her works were then sold in a variety of galleries and on the Internet.

There are many ways of expressing creativity. Not everyone is a potential Picasso, Shakespeare, or Mozart. In your 3 Personal Year, look for ways of being creative in each of your Key Life Sectors. By the same token, just because you enjoy music, or painting, or writing, it doesn't necessarily follow that in your next 3 Personal Year you will be discovered as the next Beethoven, Degas, or J. K. Rowling. Your luck will come through if you have paid your dues. Of course, that's stating the obvious, you say. But you'd be surprised at the number of people who believe they will one day suddenly, somehow be discovered, without ever having to develop their talents or skills.

Unleashing Your Creative Power

Over the years, I've often heard the words: "One day, I'm going to write a book," or "One day I'll learn to play the guitar, or take singing lessons, or learn to paint…" The list is endless. I don't know about you, but my calendar still says Monday, Tuesday, Wednesday, Thursday, Friday, Saturday, and Sunday, and… Guess what? No "one day." The closest you'll ever get to that elusive "one day" is probably the 3 Personal Year. This is when you are most likely to feel free to express yourself.

Unless applied directly to your business, artistic and creative activities usually do not generate income, at least not in the short term, so mostly they will be relegated to the pile of not-so-important things to do. Even if you have no plans for selling your artwork, or publishing, or performing, or selling your refinished old desk, or patenting your invention, creative self-expression is in and of itself a richly rewarding experience. If you should decide to incorporate a creative outlet into your life, an effective way to do this is to set aside specific time slots in your agenda for this activity. Begin by determining a schedule that is appropriate for your craft. Make this time sacrosanct. Many writers do their best work early in the morning. Painters may prefer early afternoons, for lighting, and budding musicians might enjoy strumming their guitar in the quiet late-night hours. Find a time that works for you.

Create an environment that is conducive to your craft, free of noise, clutter, and distractions. Feed the kids and the cat, walk the dog, return your mother's call, or pay that late bill before you enter your sacred creative space. Make yourself a pot of coffee or tea, and turn off the phone. Make certain your workspace is ergonomic. Don't read your email and, of course, ignore text messages during your creative time. These can wait. It's your time now. Hang a sign on your door that says *Genius at Work: Do not Disturb*. Depending on your craft, you may want to set a mood with music. Don't be hesitant to let people know that this activity is important to you.

Once you begin the process of creating, your creative juices will naturally be unleashed. This creative energy will infuse all of your thought processes and you might even see creative possibilities all around you. You may need to rein yourself in if your creativity causes you to become scattered and lose focus. Once unleashed, you may find that you get your most brilliant ideas at the most inopportune times. Don't risk losing a morsel of your brilliance. Keep a notebook, sketchbook, tablet, or recording device handy. A tiny germ of an idea could eventually grow into a significant line of thought, and tiny germs are so easily lost. Above all, relax and enjoy the process. It doesn't really matter whether or not your work is published, performed, or sold. Your creativity alone will take you on an incredible journey of self-discovery. You will discover aspects of yourself that would otherwise never have seen the light of day. Your creative process will in effect transform you.

The 3 Personal Year Month by Month

JANUARY (4 Personal Month): Work, Progress, Organization

It may be best to not plan a vacation this month. This creative year begins with a month of hard work. Your drive and focus combined with a positive attitude inspire others to follow suit. If you want to ensure that this year is as productive as possible, create a fun action plan for important projects and goals. Get yourself organized and eliminate time wasters from your life. A 3 Personal Year can be fun and exciting, but at the same time quite distracting, or even chaotic. With a solid plan in place, you can always use it to nudge yourself back in line if you do become sidetracked. Be practical, attend to details, make sensible dietary choices, and schedule regular exercise. Establish a healthy daily routine early in the year, before things become too hectic. Your creativity will have a solid foundation on which to build.

FEBRUARY (5 Personal Month): Expansion, Change, Freedom

This month can prove to be somewhat chaotic, as surprises and unexpected events arise, requiring that you be flexible with your planning. Be aware of a tendency to become sidetracked, or a desire to venture off course a bit. Keep your long-term goals in mind; refer to your action plan, while allowing yourself the chance to explore new possibilities as they arise. This is a social time, with new opportunities for growth and expansion. However, avoid impulsive or irresponsible choices or behaviour. There may be a tendency for excesses of food, or overindulging in pleasurable activities. Enjoy your free time, travel, take a vacation, and have some fun. Don't take on more responsibilities than you can handle this month. Be creative.

MARCH (6 Personal Month): Responsibility, Service, Healing

This month brings attention to events and situations involving family and those for whom you are usually responsible. People are likely to reach out to you for a variety of reasons, and if you work in a service-related field, you will be very busy. It is easy for you to communicate your thoughts clearly, and you may benefit by using creative approaches to resolve problems. Do take some time out for your own healing and self-care. Be attentive to others, and willing to be of help. Maintain a giving, non-judgmental, and compassionate attitude. Avoid interfering in the affairs of others. In the middle of your responsibilities, you may want to squeeze in a little romantic time with that special someone in your life. Remain balanced in all sectors of activity, but also in your relationships.

CHAPTER 6 · THE 3 PERSONAL YEAR

APRIL (7 Personal Month): Reflection, Analysis, Solitude

The energy of the number 7 requires that you take some time out for meditation and inner reflection or simply enjoying quiet activities such as reading, gardening, or going for long walks in the park. Since this is a 3 Personal Year, a year of creative self-expression and heightened mental activity, this is a good time to explore an artistic outlet such as journaling, drawing, or painting to help release those inner messages and inspirations. Reflect on how you can best use your creativity throughout the rest of this year. You could be feeling less inclined to go out and socialize, seeking a pause from your busy social calendar, but you may experience an endless flow of creative ideas. Despite your need for solitude, remain in touch with those who are close.

MAY (8 Personal Month): Accomplishment, Power, Action

Using creative approaches, you can make excellent progress in business and career this month. You have earned the respect of your superiors and now is the time to collect the rewards. The relationships you built in your previous 2 Personal Year are starting to pay off. Combine enthusiasm, optimism, and self-confidence to create business opportunities. This is a power month, time to push forward with your plans, take advantage of opportunities. Pursue practical and realistic goals, but at the same time remain organized, while being bold and daring. This could be a good month for money and finances. You may feel as though luck is on your side. Your positive attitude opens doors and invites the support of others.

JUNE (9 Personal Month): Completion, Endings, Release

It's time to finish off projects and bring closure where required. Review your goals for the year. Are you on track, or did you get sidetracked? If you have set short- to medium-term goals for yourself, measure your progress and make adjustments as needed. It often happens in a 3 Personal Year that we become distracted and get involved in projects that are not quite in keeping with our long-term goals. Take a close look at how you are spending your time and resources. Do a little housecleaning. Get rid of what isn't working or what isn't important. It is not unusual to feel a little lost, or emotional in a 9 Personal Month. Remain compassionate and understanding. Spend some time helping others, taking the focus off yourself. Be patient. Get some rest. A new cycle begins next month.

JULY (1 Personal Month): Self-Expression, Energy, Enthusiasm

The blues you may have been feeling last month are gone now and you feel reinvigorated, energetic, and enthusiastic again. You can find new ways of expressing yourself, and if you have creative or artistic projects on the go, you will feel inspired to produce new work. Take advantage of the opportunities presented through your social network. This is the time to go for it. Explore and express your uniqueness. You may feel ready to make important changes, to break out of your routine, or even move away from an unrewarding job or start your own business. If you have not yet explored your creativity, you may have the urge to journal or write, or even sing or dance. Your social calendar fills up again and you are drawn to new activities.

AUGUST (11/2 Personal Month): Receptivity, Inspiration, Patience

You may be feeling a little Phase II effect following your burst of energy and enthusiasm of last month. Keep in mind that self-doubt is common, especially if you have made some important changes in your personal or professional life in the past year. Stay focused and wait for projects to develop in their own time. You are particularly sensitive this month, and should protect yourself from any negative influences. Avoid discussing your new plans with those who could criticize and talk you out of them. You feel inspired, but at the same time you may feel anxious, nervous, and fragile. Nurture your inspiration. You could come up with unique solutions for the problems of someone in your environment.

SEPTEMBER (3 Personal Month): Creativity, Joie de Vivre

This month brings the year to a peak of social and creative activity. You feel inclined to reach out and express yourself in your work, through your art, and with others. Your enthusiasm is at an all-time high, and you inspire others with your optimism and cheery good nature. Focus on the more creative aspects of your work; try new approaches, express yourself freely and joyfully. If you are still uncertain about your projects, be careful not to fall in the trap of excessive analysis and criticism. Keep a positive attitude. Make new contacts, explore new networking opportunities, renew or nurture existing friendships. Take time out for enjoyment. Have a dinner party; celebrate the abundance of the autumn harvest. Oh, and stick to your budget!

OCTOBER (4 Personal Month): Organization, Discipline, Focus

With the 4 Personal Year rapidly approaching, you could be starting to feel the pressure of work and heavy obligations weighing you down. Contrary to this year, which brought out opportunities for self-expression, joy, and socialization, next year will require much more focus and attention to work. Use your creative ideas to organize yourself so that you don't have to fuss over details. Organize your workspace so that it is efficient and also pleasant to be in, especially if you foresee spending many hours there. Take care of your health. Maintain that enthusiasm and positive attitude as you get down to business. Find joy in being organized and disciplined, knowing that the hard work will pay off with tangible results in the next year.

NOVEMBER (14/5 Personal Month): *The Unexpected, Change, Travel*

You may need to rein in your impatience and restlessness this month. Keep in mind that a 4 Personal Year is only a couple of months away, and will require much focus and concentration. Resist the urge to quit, or make impulsive decisions. Just because things don't seem to be moving as quickly as you would like them to doesn't mean they aren't going at the pace they are meant to be going. Be patient. Don't make radical moves unless you are absolutely certain they are right for you. Stick to some level of routine, and avoid erratic behaviour. Take the time to learn from your errors. To keep focused on your goals and tasks, offer yourself a reward for each level of completion. Keep some free time in your schedule so as not to feel overly trapped with obligations.

DECEMBER (6 Personal Month): *Love, Relationships, Harmony*

You will likely enjoy a wonderful, fun-filled holiday season with family and friends this year. Your creative inspiration and joie de vivre expressed throughout this 3 Personal Year could extend to lavish dinner parties and social gatherings. A close friend or family member may need your support. Your sense of responsibility runs high, and feelings of love and caring are strong. This is a rewarding time, especially for relationships, business, finances, and career. You will want to establish a little balance and harmony this month, needing a little more peaceful time than you have been experiencing over the hectic past couple of months. Most likely, this will be a fine ending to a creative and fun year.

Exercise 1: Preparing for Your 3 Personal Year

1. Relative to your Life Path, Birth Day number, and personal experience of the number 3, do you feel that you have sufficient avenues for expressing your creativity? Keep in mind that you don't have to be a Picasso to be creative. Each of us has a creative genius deep inside. Are you expressing your ideas freely in your work? At home? In your leisure activities?

2. Revisit the last time you experienced a 3 Personal Year. What was going on in your life at that time? Were you able to let go and have fun? Were you able to develop a positive attitude toward life? How did you express your creativity? Did you have a tendency to be distracted or disorganized? How were your relationships and your social life?

3. Relative to where you are in your life at this time, how would you like to see your life improved and more fun? For example, if you are a workaholic 4 or 8 Life Path, have you forgotten how to laugh and enjoy life? When was the last time you took your partner on a date? Your family on a vacation? Went out for a show? Which areas of your life require more of your creative input?

4. Review your Key Life Sectors list. Are all these sectors still relevant in your life at this time? Are fun and play included among your Key Life Sectors? How about creativity, entertainment, romance? If not, make any necessary changes or adjustments.

5. Identify a sector in your life where you feel you would like to express yourself more freely, more creatively. This can be for business, home, family, or pleasure. If you have never expressed your creativity, try taking up journaling, sketching, or even singing in the car. You'd be surprised at how liberating it can feel to free your voice and sing along with your favourite song.

6. Work on improving your communication skills. In all areas, focus on expressing your true thoughts and desires. Network, socialize, and meet people. Don't stay shut up in your home. Go out; enjoy the company of friends and family. Go out on a limb, and have a dinner party. Join a networking group, or volunteer for social events at a local community center.

7. Relax and above all, learn to laugh. If you need an attitude adjustment, focus on the positive. Watch comedies, read funny books or comics. Read books on the power of positive thinking. Find ways of bringing joy into your daily life. This may seem silly, but there are so many people who have forgotten the art of simply enjoying life.

Exercise 2: Year-End Review

1. In what ways did you bring more joy into your life this year? Did you manifest your creativity? Did you free up your self-expression? In what ways did you expand your social spheres?

2. What are the benefits of these changes?

3. What is the most important lesson you learned this year?

4. What new knowledge will you bring into your upcoming 4 Personal Year?

CHAPTER 7

The 4 Personal Year

Dedication, Focus, Organization

There are three keywords that accurately describe the tone of the 4 Personal Year: work, work, and more work! Whether you like it or not, this year you will find that your energies will be best spent attending to the details and responsibilities of home, family, and work. This is not a time for grand ideas, making a big splash, or fast and furious growth and expansion. Essentially, you will need to focus on the meat-and-potatoes matters.

Last year, a 3 Personal Year, brought some exciting new ideas, perhaps a little shaking-up of your social life, some romance, a little fun, and no doubt a broad variety of experiences. Moving into the 4 energy is a bit like adding a fourth leg to a three-legged chair. It has a stabilizing effect. However, this stabilization means that you won't be able to wander off and give in to distractions, at least for a while. If you allowed yourself to be scattered and veered off course last year, now you will have the opportunity to get back on track.

You have just begun the second phase of your 9-Year Epicycle, the productive phase. You could be feeling a sense of urgency, a growing desire to accomplish something tangible, to make things happen. Last year, your mind was filled with ideas. You may have shared some of these great ideas with friends. It's time now to pass from ideas to action. This year your projects take form and become real. Whatever you set in motion at the start of this epicycle should be showing signs of life. If you started a new business, you will need to concentrate on bookkeeping, organization, and generating income. You will know where your business stands, and if your foundation is solid, you should begin to see some substantial results. Even if you haven't reached your goals, you will know that you are very much on your way. This year should move you forward significantly.

On the other hand, if your new ideas of the past couple of years lacked substance, then they are not likely to survive. You could find yourself going back to the drawing board, looking for a new way to earn a living. If this is the case, you may find that your options are limited. You will have to work very hard to find something satisfactory.

The 4 Personal Year can be a very productive year if you accept to dedicate yourself, focus, and commit to your vision. Concentrate on the details and the groundwork. Revise your budget, track your spending and earnings, and invest time, energy, and resources wisely. This can be a good year for earning and stabilizing income. Sustained effort, perseverance, and discipline will help you not only overcome obstacles, but also build a solid foundation for your future accomplishments. The work you do now may lack glamour and may at times seem to be going nowhere, but it is certain to contribute to your achievement in the 8 Personal Year, the peak of the cycle. Keep in mind that the years flow organically from one to the next, each year contributing a unique element toward the fulfillment of your goals. During the 4 Year in particular, you can make significant, tangible progress.

This will be a difficult year if you refuse to buckle down and focus on the work at hand. If you are not accustomed to discipline and hard work, you could become resentful about the restrictions and limitations you encounter when dealing with your responsibilities and duties. The 4 is the most grounded number and requires a realistic approach. It's not time for fantasy and pie-in-the-sky daydreaming. Things will go much more smoothly if you get real with yourself.

CHAPTER 7 • THE 4 PERSONAL YEAR

If you feel overwhelmed with details and obligations, revise your plan. Trim back the fat. Make a smaller garden. Make fewer promises. Walk; don't run. There is no law that says you have to do it all, at least not all in one year, nor in one 9-Year Epicycle. Many people have difficulty lowering their expectations, downsizing, and slowing down. A 4 Personal Year requires a lean and mean management style. Focus on essentials. Delegate or simply abandon what is superfluous. Fatigue and stress-related health issues can surface in a 4 Year. Be reasonable in all areas, and in particular, ensure a proper diet and get some exercise.

In a 4 Personal Year, home and family obligations can become a priority. A typical 4 Year often involves time and money spent renovating or decorating a home. Young adults leave home and rooms are reassigned. You may want to reorganize your workspace, make it more ergonomic or more efficient. This is a great time to hire a personal organizer and to clear your work and living spaces of clutter. A good system will make your work easier and more fun.

It's not uncommon to tend to the needs of an aging parent or ailing family member in a 4 Year. At the age of 73, Denise found herself caring full-time for her husband of fifty years. He had developed a severe case of shingles following a series of chemotherapy treatments for a rare blood cancer and required round-the-clock care. Denise could barely leave the house long enough to buy groceries. Although she attended to her husband's needs without a word of complaint, at the end of that 4 Year, she was clearly exhausted.

Organize your personal and business matters now so you can effectively make plans for the expansion and renewed activity you will experience next year, a 5 Personal Year. Refusing to accept responsibility at this time can lead to poor preparation and eventually to missed opportunities. Avoid wallowing in self-pity and complaints. Face your responsibilities head on, and deal with the issues that are in front of you. After all, you put yourself in your current position.

By taking charge and dealing with issues directly, you will feel empowered. Consolidate your activities. This is not a time for wastefulness. Use your resources wisely. Make the best of what you have. You should have all the tools you need at your disposal at this time to set yourself up for future success. Settle down, put down some roots, put your nose to the grindstone, and take care of business. Here is an opportunity to get the job done and actually enjoy the work. This can be a very productive year.

If you have a 4 among your core numbers, a 4 Life Path, for example, you may be quite comfortable with this focused energy, because it feels familiar and safe. At the same time, you might want to guard against being overly rigid and driving yourself into a rut. Routine may feel safe and comfortable, but in the long term, it can prevent you from taking on new challenges and limit your growth potential. A healthy balance of focus and flexibility will help you derive more from your opportunities this year.

My clients often missed their annual appointments in their 4 Personal Years, unless their birthday fell at the end of the year, at which point they generally came with their tongue hanging down to their chins, exhausted and often discouraged from the seemingly endless amount of work that had somehow piled up in their lives. They all agreed that the 4 Year was one of hard work!

Yet at the same time, it's possible to lose focus and become overly caught up with the job and money in a 4 Personal Year. Niki, a 3 Life Path with a 3 Birth Day had taken up singing early in her previous Epicycle. She had cut a CD and experienced a few club gigs, but her career as a jazz singer didn't generate enough income to justify quitting her day job. In her 4 Personal Year, she focused all her time and energy on her demanding management job, leaving no time for music. Toward the end of the year, she realized that she had reached a plateau. Although it paid well, her job did not give her the satisfaction that singing in front of an audience gave her. She decided to look for a less demanding job, one that would allow her the opportunity to spend more time on her true passion.

CHAPTER 7 • THE 4 PERSONAL YEAR

Celebrate Adversity… It May Be the Key to Your Success!

Your greatest enemy may very well be the one thing you long for the most in life: ease. Ah yes… the easy life, the good life, a life of peace and quiet. Wouldn't it be nice to never have to struggle, to never have to deal with problems on a daily basis, to never have to fight for what you want? Sounds like a nice thought, right? But is a life of ease and comfort an asset, or a liability? If you were not required to work for a living, would you? If you didn't have to overcome personal and professional challenges, would you still work your way up the competitive career ladder? If you didn't have to push yourself, would you develop your abilities? Can an athlete qualify for the Olympics without rigorous training?

From what I saw over the years in my consultation practice, most people don't move much unless they are faced with some form of challenge, either from pain, dissatisfaction, or adversity. For some reason or other, we seem to be hard-wired that way. Sometimes, it takes a really difficult period, one during which all the important aspects of life seem to be in crisis at the same time: divorce, loss of job, dealing with a troubled teen, or an illness. Only then do we cry out "Stop! There's got to be a better way," and only then will we get up and do something about it.

Surprisingly, during the easy periods we are less likely to reach within our depths and pull out our talents and abilities and express the best of ourselves. Sad, but true. When things are easy, we slack off. When times are tough, we express a wide range of responses, which can include indignation, anger, discouragement, fear, sadness, panic, anxiety, and the ever-popular, self-pity. Never did I hear a client exclaim, after being made aware of an upcoming challenging transit, "Hurray, here comes a great opportunity for me to push myself beyond my comfort zone, to learn about myself and to grow, to hone my skills and become a better person! I think I will go out and celebrate my number 4 Personal Year of hard work. Bring it on!"

How many times has an opportunity for growth, learning, and self-betterment crossed your path? Probably a lot more times than you realize. Tragedies such as the death of a loved one, illness, or loss of employment all provide you with such opportunities, but so do the simple circumstances of your day-to-day life, such as an encounter with an angry client, a misunderstanding with your spouse or child, or a traffic jam that makes you late for an important meeting. Whether big or small, each challenge provides an opportunity for learning and growth. A typical 4 Personal Year provides an abundance of challenges, some big, some small, but all requiring your dedication, focus, and attention.

The important thing to remember is that life comes from within, not from without. It isn't determined by the boulders you encounter along the way, but rather by the way you think of and then deal with these obstacles. Your life is the result of the choices you make, and these choices are based on several things, including an understanding of yourself, an understanding of the nature of life and its cycles, your willingness to tap into your resources, both inner and outer, and your readiness to accept full responsibility for your decisions.

The next time you are faced with adversity, whether major or minor, you might stop and ask yourself, *What can I learn from this situation? How can I grow? How can I become a better version of myself? How can I be more productive, a better contributor to the world around me? What can I do to help the situation at hand?* In other words, don't shrink from adversity and lie in waiting for the easy way. You'll likely stagnate. And the next time a big boulder falls on your path, gather up your friends and go out and celebrate; the most challenging times are the ones that will provide you with the greatest opportunities for growth!

CHAPTER 7 • THE 4 PERSONAL YEAR

The 4 Personal Year Month by Month

JANUARY (5 Personal Month): New Opportunities, Change

Your last year, a 3 Personal Year, may have brought you many opportunities to enjoy life, and you could be feeling the trend continuing this month. Take your time in deciding on any new endeavours, especially if you aren't one hundred percent certain of your choice. Avoid hasty decisions. Things may not be as they appear on the surface. This is a year of focus and hard work, so pick your battles carefully. You will be stuck dealing with many details over the next several months. Be prepared to work hard. You may wonder if all this work is worth the effort. You could make an interesting new business contact this month. Do take some free time off, perhaps a weekend getaway. The break will recharge your batteries and prepare you for the work ahead.

FEBRUARY (6 Personal Month): Nurturing, Balance, Harmony

If you take the time to organize your home and family life this month, things will run more smoothly throughout the year. Set up a calendar to schedule chores; share responsibilities with all members of the household. This will leave you with more time to spend together. A little affection and TLC will go a long way in providing you with the support and encouragement you need now. Your efforts at work are recognized and you may take on additional management responsibilities. People come to you for advice and support. Maintain balance and harmony in your life. Take on a fun project with your partner or children. The 4 and 6 combination is perfect for applying feng shui to your home or work space, as well as tending to your health and body needs.

MARCH (7 Personal Month): Pause, Reflection, Solitude

This is a good time to pause and reflect on your goals. Are you on track, or have you been distracted over the past few months? Take the time for research and study. Revise your plan. Are your goals realistic? Keep in mind that this is a 4 Personal Year, and you should be tending to the essentials. Are you managing your time well? You may be able to solve complex problems with simple, practical solutions. Delegate some of the more menial tasks and spend some time in quiet thought. You are not feeling particularly sociable this month. You'd probably rather figure out how to fix that leaky faucet than go out and party. Your search for the meaning of life may be stirred as your mind travels deeper into your inner self. You could receive important insights. Keep in mind that there are no real problems, only solutions awaiting discovery.

APRIL (8 Personal Month): Power, Results, Advancement

If you have paid attention to details and focused on the work at hand, this month should be very rewarding, both personally and professionally. This is when dedication and hard work pay off. You feel on top of your game now, and the results are showing that your efforts have been worth it. More than ever, you are focused and determined to reach your goals. This is an excellent month for advancement on all levels, especially professionally and financially. Go for your goals. Being in a 4 Year, remember to keep both feet on the ground and remain practical. There is much work yet to be done this year. Proceed with confidence; this is a time of great material accomplishment. You are focused on career issues this month, and family is likely to take a back seat.

MAY (9 Personal Month): Completion, Endings, Release

You may find relief as a work project reaches completion this month. Having worked hard over the past few months, you could be feeling a bit tired and in need of a break. If you can't manage a vacation, try to take some time off, even if it is only a long weekend. Put your feet up; go for a long drive in the country. Take care of your health. Your emotions are running high, and you could find yourself overdramatizing situations, especially as you bring matters to a close. A work-related relationship may end. You could find reward in doing some community or volunteer work. Finish home projects, clean out the garage, remove clutter from your life. The better organized you are, the more productive you will be throughout the remainder of this year.

JUNE (1 Personal Month): Energy Renewal, Productivity

New work projects present themselves, or new career opportunities come to you now. Although you are inspired to move forward with your plans and perhaps even take on more work, keep in mind that progress will be slow in a 4 Personal Year and results may not be immediately visible. Your continued diligence and attention to detail will keep things moving forward. You will need to be patient this month. Keep some balance in your life, so as not to burn out. It's easy to forget about everything and throw yourself into your work, especially when you are feeling energized. To get unstuck from a rut, try a new approach and break up the monotony of your daily routine. Take a different route to work; rearrange your workspace.

JULY (11/2 Personal Month): Relationships, Intuition, Cooperation

In order to accomplish your goals, you may need to work closely with others this month. Progress may seem slow, and you may not see eye-to-eye with colleagues. Your intuition is providing you with insights that may guide you to thinking and acting "outside the box." Your colleagues or partners may not be open to progressive solutions right now, and you could feel left out or ignored. This isn't the time to take things personally. Remember, keep your eye on the ball; be realistic. Save your unique ideas for later; they will eventually find a place. Patience and cooperation are key now as you work to strengthen the relationships you need to reach your goals. Use your encounters with others to deepen your knowledge of yourself. Find guidance and comfort from within.

AUGUST (3 Personal Month): Social Life, Creativity, Practicality

Work demands might lighten a bit this month, do try to take a break, without completely losing your momentum. A vacation would give you the renewal of optimism and energy that you will need to continue with your hard work in the months that follow. If you can't take a vacation, plan a dinner party with friends at home. Take some fun time with family as well. Work on a creative or artistic project at home. Spend some time on a hobby, listening to music, or going for leisurely drives in the country. Your mind is open to down-to-earth inspiration, helping you find practical solutions to everyday problems. Harness a positive outlook by acknowledging the progress achieved this year to date. Look for creative ways of making the work more fun.

SEPTEMBER (13/4 Personal Month): Limitation, Doubt, Work

This month could prove to be a bit stressful as your workload rises substantially. This is the time to focus on details and keep your goals in mind. Draw on your feelings of optimism from last month to get you through it. Maintain a healthy diet and exercise routine. Revise your budget; curb your spending. Although things appear to be moving far more slowly than you would like, it is necessary that you focus on foundation issues. Reorganize your plan if it lacks structure. Don't overlook the more tedious, basic aspects of your work. Remind yourself that hard work unfailingly leads to rewards. You get out of life what you put into it. Now is the time to see this principle at work. Tremendous opportunities

CHAPTER 7 • THE 4 PERSONAL YEAR

are just around the corner; a solid foundation will ensure your success. Note that if this is a 22/4 Year, September will be a Basic 4 Month, so the energy is likely to feel more positive, and can be more productive. This book was revised and edited in September of a 22/4 Year. That's a lot of work! A good friend of mine, who shares the same number cycles, spent a chunk of that month sanding and staining her huge wooden deck. Being a 22/4 Life Path, she did an amazing job!

OCTOBER (5 Personal Month): Expansion, Adventure, Opportunity

You will be feeling relieved and much more free as the accumulated pressures of the previous months dissipate. If you worked hard last month, you will be ready to consider the new opportunities that are opening up before you. Remember to stay focused on your long-term goals, and to not jump on the first glossy opportunity that arises. This is an excellent time to expand your reach. Your circle of contacts grows, and your new acquaintances could be very supportive of your unique endeavours. Be flexible and open-minded. Consider new ways of doing things. Change is just around the corner. Break from the routine a bit, without losing track of your direction. The coming year will bring plenty of opportunities for growth and expansion.

NOVEMBER (6 Personal Month): Service, Responsibility, Family

Your attention may be required on the home front. A family member could require your care, assistance, or support. At work, you may be called upon to help manage complex situations. Be kind, understanding, and sympathetic as you try to find practical solutions to the problems of others. Re-establish balance and harmony in your routine if you have been drawn off track by the exciting developments of last month. This is an excellent time for creative self-expression. If you are working on an art, drama, music, or writing project, your work could progress nicely. Revise your diet and get back to your workout routine. This can be a rewarding month as your work may be recognized and highly praised.

DECEMBER (7 Personal Month): Analysis, Study, Reflection

This year of hard work and the establishing of solid foundations is drawing to a close. You can reward yourself now by measuring your progress, based on the goals you set for yourself at the start of this 9-Year Epicycle. You will need some quiet time by yourself to reflect and re-evaluate your situation. Review your long-term goals. Doing so now will prevent you from being led astray in the coming months as you move into a 5 Personal Year, a year of freedom, change, surprises, and unexpected occurrences. Spend some quiet, peaceful time in nature. Reconnect with your inner spirit. Listen for new guidance and wisdom. While you may not be much of a party animal this month, your inner peace and wisdom will naturally flow outward to everyone you encounter.

Exercise 1: Preparing for Your 4 Personal Year

1. Relative to your Life Path, Birth Day number, and personal experience of the number 4, are you prepared to focus and work hard toward the accomplishment of your goals? Are your work and home environments well organized? For example, if you are a party-loving 3 Life Path, you may find it difficult to get focused now.

2. Go back to the last time you experienced a 4 Personal Year. What was going on in your life at that time? Did you feel limited or restricted by the obligations of your job or family? Were you well organized, or did you have trouble focusing on the work at hand? Did you experience illness?

3. Relative to where you are in your life at this time, how can you reorganize your life to make things easier, both at home

CHAPTER 7 · THE 4 PERSONAL YEAR

and at work? Having an efficient routine and being well-organized can make a 4 Personal Year more fun and feel less restrictive. A consultation with a personal organizer might be helpful.

4. Review your Key Life Sectors list. Are all these sectors relevant in your life at this time? If not, make any necessary changes or adjustments. In a 4 Personal Year, sometimes it is necessary to cut back on certain activities, and focus on essentials. The key is to be well organized.

5. This is a foundation year. Evaluate how you use your time. Learn how to manage your time efficiently. Eliminate time and energy wasters. You will need to focus all your attention on achieving your goals this year. Implement a system that will help you organize your priorities. Stick to your Key Life Sectors and your goals for the year.

6. Note if there are any areas in your life in which you are overly rigid. If the 4 energy is already strong in your numbers, you may need to learn to relax a bit, maintain a positive and flexible attitude, and not lose track of your responsibilities toward others.

7. Establish healthy diet and exercise habits. Do a financial check-up. Make sure your budget is up to date and reflects your current situation and needs.

Exercise 2: Year-End Review

1. In what ways did you get organized and focused this year?

2. How has this added structure improved your life?

3. What is the most important lesson you learned this year?

4. What new knowledge will you bring into your upcoming 5 Personal Year?

CHAPTER 8

The 5 Personal Year

Freedom, Change, Progress

The stabilizing force of the number 4 gets a little shaking up as you move forward into the 5 Personal Year. If you were to continue with the same demanding pace, it wouldn't be long before you found yourself entrenched in a rut of work, duty, and obligation. Over time, your interest would fade, you would lose all sense of enthusiasm, grow bored, and probably become resentful of your limitations. The addition of a 1 to the 4 changes that. In the 5 Personal Year, it's time to do a little dance and break up the routine. It's a bit like adding a fifth leg to the table, only this leg is longer. You lose your balance, and anything can happen.

Fatigue, pressures from overwork, and feelings of restriction can build up in a 4 Personal Year, so the energy of the 5 Year is usually quite welcome. It is often experienced as an increased desire for freedom, a need to loosen the holds of daily habits, and a yearning for change. This is a great year for travel and for making new acquaintances. Try to keep some free time in your weekly schedule so you can occasionally break away from the routine.

Your readiness for change as well as your need for change will determine the direction you will take this year. The years during which most major changes occur are the 1, 5, and 9 Personal Years. For each of these years, change is based on unique motivations, the 1 corresponding with a renewal of energy and new beginnings, the 5 expressing a need for freedom and adventure, and the 9 manifesting completion and release. Common events for a 5 Personal Year include important job changes, relocations, home and family moves, and a change of orientation in school.

If you are comfortable with change, that is, if you have a healthy relationship with the energy of the number 5, you will enjoy the expansion and release from the containment and limitations of last year. Your creativity will be unleashed and you will look for original ways of doing your work and reaching your goals. You will be ready for adventure and new experiences, ready to stretch yourself and do things you have never done before. This is the time to inject new elements or new activities into your projects and boldly go where you have not gone before!

If, on the other hand, you are not comfortable with the energy of the 5, if you have strong 4s or 2s for example, and prefer to hold on to old ways of doing things, you may find this year to be uncomfortably destabilizing. There is always an element of uncertainty in times of change, and whenever 5 energy is present, there are few guarantees, and often unexpected surprises can arise. No matter how solid your plan is, you cannot completely control the outcome of your choices. Sometimes, however, the injection of a new approach or new experience, even if it wasn't sought out or even desired, is just what was needed to help move things forward in ways you could not have imagined. Without change, you could miss out on important opportunities for growth, learning, and progress.

Review your long-term goals. You are halfway through the current epicycle. Make those changes that will get you significantly closer to your goals. If you established a solid foundation last year, you should be in a good position to leap forward and take certain risks. This is a great time for personal and business growth. Expand your boundaries. Explore new avenues. In a 5 Personal Year, you can benefit from the right mix of flexibility, risk, and focus. Risk and flexibility will help you explore options that you might not otherwise consider, while a clear focus on your long-term goals will help move you forward with purpose and direction.

CHAPTER 8 · THE 5 PERSONAL YEAR

The 5 energy is quite progressive, and you could find yourself coming up with ideas that are a bit ahead of their time. Remember, it is the energy of R&D, so time to experiment! You may have to practise patience until the world around you is ready for your bold new ideas. Although you may feel ready to try new ways of doing things, avoid leaping before carefully thinking things through. The 5 can indicate a tendency for exaggeration, inconsistency, and impulsiveness. Don't lose track of your responsibilities and your long-term vision. Trying new things doesn't necessarily require that you throw out the baby with the bath water.

This is a much freer energy than the 4. You could encounter the breaking up of old conditions in your life, causing the delays and limitations of the past year to slowly dissipate. Some people respond to the energy of the 5 Personal Year by giving in to long-repressed restlessness, by moving, changing jobs, or changing interests or even love relationships without giving a second thought to the consequences of their actions. Be careful to not jump ship midstream. Change for the sake of change alone can set you back rather than forward. If change is not welcome, it can be a hectic and chaotic year. If you are ready for something new, it can be an exciting year.

Your success this year will depend on your ability to make wise choices, to flow with the changing conditions of your life, to release the old and accept the new, to be adventurous and ready to take some risks, all the while keeping your long-term goals in focus. Be aware of a tendency to overindulge in the good things you enjoy. By maintaining balance, this can be a very enjoyable and fruitful year.

This is a great time for adventure and fun activities. In his 5 Personal Year, Robert, 52 and single, decided it was time to venture out and start dating. He was not interested in doing the bar scene, but some of the guys at work recommended that he try Internet dating. This was not something he would normally have done, yet, intrigued by the idea, he ventured out. This was a very exciting and rewarding time for Robert, where he learned much about dating and women, but more importantly, about himself.

Freedom from the weight of heavy responsibility doesn't always come in a happy package. If you will recall from the previous chapter, in a 4 Personal Year Denise was quite heavily burdened by the care of her ailing husband. In April of the following year, a 5 Personal Year of sudden change and a 9 Personal Month of endings and release, her husband suffered a severe stroke. Forty-eight hours later he passed away. Understandably this was a time of profound sorrow, a most traumatic moment in her life. Even though her husband had been seriously ill, she had never given up hope that he might get better. The stroke was unexpected and sudden, a typical 5 expression. While heart-breaking, this was also a time of liberation, for now she was free of her responsibilities as a full-time caregiver.

The expansiveness of the 5 energy also made this a time of much new learning for Denise, as she was plunged headfirst into the world of notaries, legal papers, taxes, finances, sorting through the complex matters of settling her husband's estate. Later on that year, she was given her first computer and Internet account, adding even more new experiences as she was shown how to surf the Internet and collect her email. In many ways, the radical energy of this 5 Personal Year pushed Denise to tap into her 3 Life Path skills like no other year before ever had.

The 5 Personal Year Month by Month

JANUARY (6 Personal Month): Relationships, Home, Family

You are no doubt anxious to break free from the limitations and restrictions of last year. A 5 Personal Year can be an exciting time, with new opportunities just around the corner. Others sense this about you, and come to you for advice, or just for the pleasure of participating in joint projects. As you bring change into your life,

CHAPTER 8 · THE 5 PERSONAL YEAR

especially home and family life, remember to do so in moderation. Others may not be ready for as much change as you are. Try to break up your routine with a little variety. Consider making your workspace more ergonomic. This is a good month to develop new personal and business relationships. Being at the start of a 5 Year, you will value your freedom more than usual, and may resent some of the responsibilities that restrict your movement.

FEBRUARY (7 Personal Month): Reflection, Meditation, Evaluation

Before things get too hectic, it might be a good idea to take some time out and review your situation, re-evaluate your goals, both long-term and short-term, and make sure you have a solid plan in place. Your restlessness for change and adventure may conflict with your need to reflect. Try to find a balance between both urges; both are necessary for your growth and development. Take advantage of this introspective time to look for new ideas through inner guidance. Deepen your understanding of your life purpose and direction. You may not be open to the input of others this month, preferring to rely on your own insights. Even though you may be certain that you are right, avoid being insensitive to the opinions of others.

MARCH (8 Personal Month): Money, Business, Finances

Career and finances take precedence over other areas of activity this month. Your focus should be on expanding and pushing your professional goals forward. However, use wisdom in making financial choices. Do your due diligence; obtain proper advice before investing money and assets. If in doubt, wait. Avoid acting on impulse, especially when under a number 5 influence. Your excessive enthusiasm could cloud your judgment. Be patient in all financial matters. Your intuition could provide you with important insights as to how to inject new energy into your career or business. You are feeling quite dynamic now, and ready to explore new avenues. This may not be the best month for family and romance.

APRIL (9 Personal Month): Endings, Completion, Release

This can be an emotional time, with projects coming to a close and a sense of urgency to finish things off. In a 5 Personal Year, you are eager for change and new experiences, but the 9 Month requires that you first release any redundant or outdated activities and preoccupations from your life. A relationship that has caused you to feel restricted may come to an end. If the 5 energy is strong in your core numbers, you may be inclined to quit a project before it is completed, just to be relieved of its burden. Think twice about bringing something to an end before you have learned its lesson. Remember it is always best to learn your way out; that way you will never doubt your decision. This is a good time to travel and take a vacation.

MAY (1 Personal Month): Renewal, Progress, Promotion

Add change and new experiences to your agenda! This is a great time to expand or promote yourself, your interests, or your business. Progress is easily accomplished now, and you are ready for new ideas and approaches. You may now use your creativity, ingenuity, and dramatic flair to get your point across, make a sale, or obtain support to get an innovative project underway. An excellent career move or opportunity is possible. This is the time to be bold and daring and to break away from old worn-out ways of doing things. You could make an exciting new acquaintance this month. If you are single, get out there and make yourself known. Try something new and different, but don't rush things. If in a relationship, be mindful of casual flirtations; instead, put some fun and romance back into your marriage. Be adventurous.

CHAPTER 8 · THE 5 PERSONAL YEAR

JUNE (11/2 Personal Month): Sensitivity, Intuition, Relationships

Bubbling with new ideas, you can derive much satisfaction by helping others with their new projects or with problem solving. You enjoy the company of colleagues and friends, especially those with whom you have shared interests. Your intuition is right on the mark and you could pick up on some interesting, innovative solutions for unexpected problems. However, be cautious with financial dealings. Your idealism and perhaps naiveté, if so inclined, may lead you in the wrong direction. There is a certain tension inside of you, an eagerness to produce something of importance. You have big dreams and you feel the need to share these with someone you trust. Open up and experience the closeness and comfort of sharing. Spend some time with someone you care for; do something different.

JULY (3 Personal Month): Joie de Vivre, Travel, Socializing

This will likely be a very enjoyable month for you, an ideal time for a vacation, or a road trip with family or friends. At work or in business, there will be plenty of opportunities for socializing and making interesting new contacts. Even though many businesses are on summer break now, take advantage of this wonderful social trend to enjoy leisure and fun activities with prospective clients and business acquaintances. Why not take up tennis or sailing? Join a cycling group; sign up for a golf tournament. This is a fortunate time for you and you could find yourself in the right place, at the right time. If you have a creative outlet, channel some of your inspiration into this activity. Use your talents now; they will serve you well. Take advantage of opportunities to share your innovative ideas.

AUGUST (13/4 Personal Month): Work, Work, Work

Well, it's time to pay the piper! Hopefully, you took some time off to rest and enjoy yourself last month. You'll have to get serious and attend to those details and work matters that you have been putting off for a while now. This is not a good month for a vacation! If you refuse to accept the work that is in front of you, you could be short-changing yourself in the future. This is a foundation and bottom-line month. Focus on the important issues, the details, most likely those activities or tasks you've been cleverly avoiding. You can't ignore them forever! Work on those pesky little home projects that have been hanging around a long time. Better yet, gather your best patience and approach them like R&D projects!

SEPTEMBER (14/5 Personal Month): Freedom, Change, Surprises

If you worked hard last month, you will be rewarded with very interesting and exciting opportunities for growth and change. Always with your long-term plan in mind, explore new opportunities and prepare for change. If you have an abundance of number 5 energy among your numbers, you could be inclined to excessive restlessness and impatience or over-indulging in your favourite activities. This month requires that you be flexible and open to change and new experiences, while keeping an eye on the ball. New relationships begun now may not be sustained in the long term. Release the old, go with the new, but use good judgment in all decisions. Avoid making hasty decisions. Change for the sake of change alone may not be wise.

OCTOBER (6 Personal Month): Responsibility, Family, Balance

Family matters come to the fore as the 6 Personal Year approaches. If, despite your best efforts, you took on too much or veered off track last month, now is the time to pull yourself together and

CHAPTER 8 • THE 5 PERSONAL YEAR

re-establish balance in your life. Enjoy the support, caring, and nurturing of family and friends. Plan a family get-together. Focus on diet and exercise. You may feel the crunch of added responsibility, especially from new projects or areas of activity that have recently been brought into your life. You will find pleasure in being helpful to others. A new acquaintance could bring much joy into your life. Prepare for a more moderate pace of life coming in the new year.

NOVEMBER (16/7 Personal Month): Reflection, Meditation, Analysis

It's time to take a serious look at where you have been, where you are, and where you are going. You may not be ready for such intense introspection, following a year of freedom, change, and opportunity. Perhaps you feel somewhat isolated, or different, as though others don't really understand you. Taking the time out to reflect could bring you much inner growth. Do research or background work. Make certain you are properly informed about the new areas of activity you have taken on in recent months. Reconnect with your inner guidance. Is the direction of your life in tune with your innermost desires? Are you living your passion? Are you pursuing your true life purpose? You may feel a little reclusive this month. Stay in tune with the needs of loved ones.

DECEMBER (8 Personal Month): Accomplishment, Power, Business

This month could bring an exciting new business opportunity that would help move your career interests forward. Your focus is likely to be more on money and business rather than on family and leisure this month. Keep in mind that the 6 Personal Year is just around the corner, so it will be important for you to establish balance in all aspects of your life. Make choices and changes that will facilitate harmony in your personal as well as professional relationships. You've had enough adventure and excitement this year to keep you motivated for a while! You are feeling more confident and empowered now. This is a great period of personal accomplishment. You could be rewarded for a job well done. This is a favourable month for career, money matters, and finances.

Exercise 1: Preparing for Your 5 Personal Year

1. Relative to your Life Path, Birth Day number, and personal experience of the number 5, are you ready to stretch yourself, be adventurous, and take on new challenges? If you are a strong 4, for example, you may find it difficult to deal with the unexpected occurrences and surprises that are common in a 5 Personal Year.

2. Revisit the last time you experienced a 5 Personal Year. What was going on in your life at that time? What changes did you make? Did you experience chaos, or measured progress and growth?

3. Relative to where you are in your life at this time, where would you like to see progress and growth? If you've had difficulty managing change in the past, how will you approach change now? How can you introduce change while maintaining an eye on your goals? How will change bring you closer to your goals?

4. Review your Key Life Sectors list. Are all these sectors relevant in your life at this time? Where is change most needed?

5. In what ways could you stretch yourself now, by trying something new, doing something different? Keep in mind that new experiences keep the brain healthy and the spirit youthful. What new skills would you like to learn?

6. While making changes, experimenting, and enjoying adventure, keep an eye on your long-term goals. Ensure continued progress in the right direction by aligning your actions with your values and your goals. Use creative and original ways

for setting goals, such as maintaining a storyboard or scrapbook with pictures representing each of your goals.

7. If you are inclined to making radical decisions, take a deep breath, and think things through. Do your due diligence in all risky ventures. Are these changes appropriate? Are they necessary? Will they move you closer to your long-term goals? What will be the impact of these changes on your personal life? Your family life? Your professional life?

Exercise 2: Year-End Review

1. In what ways did your life change this year? How did you stretch yourself, expand your field of experience?

2. What are the benefits of these changes?

3. What is the most important lesson you learned this year?

4. What new knowledge will you bring into your upcoming 6 Personal Year?

CHAPTER 9

The 6 Personal Year

Harmony, Responsibility, Balance

After the excitement and rapid progress of the 5 Personal Year, you may be ready to settle down a bit, catch your breath, and perhaps even find your bearings if last year put you in a tailspin. The addition of a 1 to the 5 energy establishes a new level of balance and provides opportunities for increased rewards through service to others, career advancement, and improved personal health and inner peace.

The 6 Personal Year brings attention to family and home life, and in particular, to all your responsibilities for others, whether at home, in the community, or in the workplace. While people express their increased need for your attention and help, you benefit from the comfort and support of home and family. Above all else, this year it is important that you re-establish a sense of balance in your life, otherwise you could feel overwhelmed with the burden of responsibility. People may need you more than ever now. They call on your knowledge and expertise; they make demands on your emotional and personal resources, including time, energy, and money.

Although the 6 is a number of service and responsibility, it is important to balance the time you spend in the service of others so as not to grow resentful of the demands made upon you. If you have 6s among your core numbers, you may already have a tendency to do too much for others. If this is the case, then this may be a good time to learn that sometimes it's okay and even very healthy for all concerned to simply say no. In fact, doing too much for others can have the effect of taking power away from them, and they in turn can become offended by your meddling, even if it is well intentioned.

If you lack 6 energy, you could become resentful of your increasing responsibilities. Be honest with yourself and with others; only make those promises you know you can keep. Often it is better to promise less and deliver more than to constantly make promises that are never kept. Honesty and integrity will go a long way toward solidifying relationships this year. Honour your commitments to others and you will receive the respect of others in return.

Relationships that were developed and nurtured in your previous 2 Personal Year could bear fruit now, and you may benefit from the protection and support of those whom you have served well in the past. During a 6 Personal Year, it is not uncommon to receive recognition from your peers or superiors for a job well done. You could become involved in teaching, coaching, counselling, advising, or mediating and peacemaking in work or domestic situations. While helping others resolve their problems, do not neglect your family and friends. At the same time, you do not need to be a martyr. Your keyword for the year should be *balance*, in all things.

Unlike last year, this is a year of moderate but steady growth and advancement. Focus on the issues that are close at hand. Complete projects and activities as they present themselves. Avoid procrastination. If you are well organized, settling into your roles and responsibilities should be relatively easy, and you will shine in your function, especially if you have a management role. Take care of settling bills, banking, and estate matters, as well as long-term financial plans this year.

You will feel the need for close, personal relationships, and if single, could find love knocking at your door. Your nesting urge could kick in and you may want to start a family. Settling down, getting married, and attending to the details of everyday life has

CHAPTER 9 • THE 6 PERSONAL YEAR

a certain appeal now. This is a time for consolidating personal relationships and for emotional grounding. It is an excellent year for marriage, love, and romance. If you have some unresolved issues in a personal relationship, now would be a good time to get some help in the form of counselling, or to do some research on the subject of relationships.

You will seek and enjoy giving and receiving affection. You strive for balance, harmony, serenity, and beauty in your surroundings as well as in your relationships. Home or domestic responsibilities require your attention and you could buy or rent a home, renovate a property, buy furniture, paint, or decorate. This is the perfect time to use feng shui to bring more harmony in your home and work environments. I actually refer to 6 as the number of feng shui: applied balance and harmony in all areas of life.

If you think a normal happy family is not for you, keep in mind that when the timing is right, things somehow manage to fall into place. Peter came to see me when he was twenty-five years old, in a 9 Personal Year. His charts indicated a sensitive, caring personality, typical of a 2 Life Path person. He had tremendous potential for working with people, in a counselling capacity or in the community in areas such as social work or police work. At the time, all these options seemed to be closed to him. He supported himself with a full-time job in shipping, had debts to pay off, and no family he could call on for help. Not academically inclined, and with only a high school diploma, higher education was out of the question. In his youth, he had gotten into trouble with drugs and the law. He was a recovering addict, and had a criminal record. By all appearances, social work and police work were out of the question. Yet he knew that his job was unsatisfactory, and in the long run he would have to find something more fulfilling.

I studied his charts for some idea of how he might express some of his talents, even in a minor way, so that at the end of the day he would feel a certain degree of satisfaction. It's not given to every person to find complete fulfillment in their day job. Sometimes, a job is simply necessary for survival, a means to an end. Many people find contentment in their personal life, in their function as caregivers for family and friends, through some form of creative self-expression, or through involvement in the community.

Peter had some clear talents and abilities, but appeared to be faced with nothing but closed doors. I could see that he wouldn't be happy in the long run in his current situation, even if he did move up the ranks and acquire more authority or management responsibilities. During our conversation, he expressed having a dream of working with adolescents who had trouble with drugs and the law, much as he had experienced a few years earlier. Looking for a way for him to tap into his natural inclinations and stir up feelings of personal satisfaction, I suggested that he volunteer a few hours a week at a local youth support organization. That way, I explained, he would be using some of his talents and satisfying a very real and unexpressed need to help others, the natural expression of his 2 Life Path.

Peter phoned me just before Christmas, two years later. By then he was at the end of a 2 Personal Year. Shyly, he mentioned his name, asking if I remembered him. Of course, I did. How could I forget such a remarkably kind and caring young man! He had called to tell me that he had taken my advice and found volunteer work at a youth group downtown. He had volunteered with this group for eighteen months, at which point, given his natural ability for the work, the director offered him a full-time position. At an age where most youth are out partying and having a good time, facing seemingly insurmountable obstacles, this young man followed his heart, put himself in the flow of his natural talents and abilities, and caused the tide of opportunities to turn in his favour. A few years later, in the 6 Personal Year, he found love, married and had his first child. By putting himself on his true path, he aligned himself with the opportunities that flowed as natural consequences of his actions.

CHAPTER 9 · THE 6 PERSONAL YEAR

Sometimes it takes tremendous courage and faith in yourself to actively pursue the dreams you were born to follow. They don't have to be big dreams, as was the case with Peter. He wasn't likely to become a billionaire on a social worker's salary, but he was following his true purpose, and in so doing, he was making a significant difference in the lives of many troubled young souls.

After being plunged into a series of adventures and new experiences in her 5 Personal Year, Denise, whose story we began in the chapter on the 4 Personal Year, received a call for help from her sister. In her 6 Personal Year, Denise made several trips to a town 3 hours away to help her sister following leg and arm surgery that had left her incapable of taking care of herself. With her help, her sister recovered remarkably well. The 6 often requires that you set your own needs aside for the sake of others.

Although the 6 Year is generally experienced as positive, favouring home and family relationships, if you have some unresolved issues with family or if you have not come to terms with your responsibilities toward others, this can be a difficult year. Ivan, a highly sensitive 11/2 Life Path, found himself out of work in his 6 Personal Year. Feeling different or in some way special, a common trait of the 11/2 energy, he turned down job opportunities or failed job interviews. He was either over-qualified, or under-experienced. His wife was pressuring him to get a job and pull his weight. They had lost their home and were living in a relative's house. During that year, Ivan could not see beyond his own specialness and failed to set aside his needs for those of his wife and daughter, creating additional tension. It was a very unsettling time during which he lost not only his job, but also nearly lost his marriage. Unlike Peter, Ivan was unable to set aside his needs and thus could not benefit from the normally supportive and protective influences of the number 6.

The 6 Personal Year Month by Month

JANUARY (7 Personal Month): Reflection, Analysis, Study

As the new year begins, you will want to spend a little more time than usual on your yearly planning and goal-setting. Above all, you realize that your life cannot continue at the same pace it did in the last year. Your key goal this year should be to establish balance and harmony in all aspects of your life. It may seem boring at first glance, but you will benefit by doing all things in good measure. You may feel a little lost right now, as the energy of the previous year winds down. You'll need some alone time this month, so take some time out, read, meditate, or spend some time in nature. Do not worry if things are not moving as quickly as you expect them to. They won't move as fast as last year, but they will move, in time. Think about how you might bring more balance and harmony in your life this year.

FEBRUARY (8 Personal Month): Power, Business, Money

Your attention will be on business, money, and career matters this month. Significant results may be achieved now. You are in an excellent position to receive recognition for a job well done. Long-standing professional relations can lead to further opportunities for advancement. If you are remembering to keep a balance between home and work, you will be able to share your achievements with family members. Tend to money matters relating to home and property. Invest in that renovation project you've been putting off. Put money aside for a family vacation later this year. Although the 6 Personal Year doesn't normally indicate big flashy accomplishments, this can be a very productive month.

MARCH (9 Personal Month): Generosity, Completion, Endings

Determine which of your responsibilities are appropriate at this point in your current epicycle. If you have strong 6 energy in your core numbers, you may be in the habit of taking on way more responsibility than is necessary or even healthy. People sense this, and can take advantage of your giving nature. Sometimes, you are not doing a person a favour by doing for them what they can be taught to do for themselves. This may be a good time for a relationship cleanup. On the other hand, you may be drawn to participate in a community or volunteer project. Your heart reaches out to others, and you are in a generous and expansive mood. In all interactions with others, patience, compassion, and understanding are called for. Keep in mind that this is a month of endings; complete or unload unfinished projects.

APRIL (1 Personal Month): Initiative, Relationships, Renewal

This would be a good time to begin a home design or decoration project or to plan an activity with family members. Your loved ones will appreciate your upbeat and energetic attitude, and you will enjoy the time spent with them. You can proceed with confidence and initiative with your plans. This is an excellent month for money, career, and personal advancement. A marriage, engagement, or renewal of a relationship commitment is also possible at this time. If you are in a difficult relationship in which issues have not been successfully worked out, this may be a good time to part ways. You feel lucky, positive, and supported now. If you are single and seeking companionship, you might meet someone special. Stir some romance into your love life.

MAY (11/2 Personal Month): Intuition, Idealism, Inspiration

The pace slows down a bit this month. You may have to wait while new projects begun last month take shape. Your intuition guides you in your dealings with family and close friends, and you may be called on to settle a misunderstanding or dispute. Your heightened sensitivity and desire for harmony allow you to find positive solutions for all concerned. Fully appreciative of your valued relationships, you find reward and comfort in domestic activities. Remain patient and allow things to develop in their own time. Avoid arguments and disputes; you may be too emotionally involved to be objective. Use tact and diplomacy in all interactions. You could benefit from inner guidance if you are open and receptive. It's time to put those antennas to work!

JUNE (3 Personal Month): Self-Expression, Creativity, Enjoyment

You will be in the mood to socialize, go out with friends, have a good time, and generally take advantage of this early summer month with fun activities. This is an excellent time for a family vacation. Even if you must work, schedule some weekend road trips, enjoy the surrounding scenery, attend an outdoor concert, engage in an outdoor sport, go strawberry picking. You could be easily distracted, so keep your calendar or your agenda handy. At the same time, be aware of a tendency for spending money. Luck is on your side now, and your upbeat and positive attitude makes you a delight to be with. This is a great time for romance. A new relationship could be blossoming nicely. Taking time out for artistic or creative projects could also be very rewarding. Have fun and enjoy yourself this month.

JULY (13/4 Personal Month): Work, Service, Discipline

Hopefully, you didn't become overly distracted last month, because now you will need to get back to work. This is certainly not the best time for rest and relaxation. You seem to be pulled in two directions with a need to pay attention to a pile of work at home on the one hand, and another healthy load in your job or business. Being organized in all areas of your life will make the work much easier to handle. Finish projects around the home, while attending to the details of work. If you are working on a renovation project, you could encounter some challenges. Maintain a positive attitude, even though you would probably rather be doing anything else but work. Spend time with family, even if you don't have time for a vacation this month. This can be a very productive month for work.

AUGUST (14/5 Personal Month): Change, Surprises, Freedom

You may be feeling the need for a little escape and adventure this month. Many responsibilities have been added to your task list this year, and you could use a little breathing room. Enjoy time out with family, do those new and unusual things you've been planning on doing but never got around to. This is an excellent time for social activities, a vacation, and for meeting new people. You will need a little free time, so try to delegate some of those less interesting responsibilities. If you can't delegate, if possible, just set them aside for the time being. Be flexible and remain prepared to accommodate surprises. Leave some spare time in your agenda. Try new approaches; be bold and daring; experiment. Sometimes, change is as good as a rest.

SEPTEMBER (6 Personal Month): Harmony, Family, Home

You will enjoy time spent with family and friends this month, and especially activities centred on the home. If you haven't established order and balance in your life, you may feel somewhat restricted by all the responsibilities that seem to be coming at you from every direction. You may even feel resentful of those who seem to make too many demands on your time and energy. If your lifestyle is balanced, you will enjoy getting involved in some community activity or family project. Devote yourself to the needs of others; set some of your own needs aside for the time being. You will be rewarded for your dedication and service. This is a good month for stepping up and taking charge at work. Tend to your health; take a day off work and do something relaxing.

OCTOBER (7 Personal Month): Analysis, Reflection, Isolation

With all the time you have spent this year in service to others, you have earned a little time out! You will very much appreciate time spent by yourself, either reading, listening to music, engaging in your favourite hobby, meditating, or being out in nature. Reflect now on the progress you've made this year; review the goals you set for yourself back in January. Adjust these goals to better suit any new developments that may have occurred over the past couple of months, if necessary. Consider your personal, home, family, and career plans for the future. You will soon be moving into a 7 Personal Year, a time when you will be drawn to focus on the more personal and intimate aspects of your life. Inner healing and growth will be your focus. Go within and look for ways of resolving any long-standing relationship issues.

NOVEMBER (8 Personal Month): Career, Money, Business

This is an excellent time for business and money matters, the culmination of your efforts as the year approaches its closing. You could make an important decision regarding a home or family matter. You have learned much about balancing home and career this year, and you are ready to implement measures that will ensure continued harmony for all concerned. This is a rewarding time, as results are finally manifesting in a tangible fashion. Tend to financial affairs, especially as they relate to home and

CHAPTER 9 • THE 6 PERSONAL YEAR

family. You could be contemplating the future of your career or business as you approach the start of a 7 Personal Year. Keep in mind that the current epicycle will peak in just over a year, in the 8 Personal Year. Focus on tangible results.

DECEMBER (9 Personal Month): Completion, Endings, Release

Finish those long-standing home projects, clean out the garage, feng shui your home; relieve yourself of clutter. Do whatever it takes to ensure balance, harmony, and peacefulness in your home and work environments. Next year, you will have lots of things on your mind, and you won't want to be bothered by mundane details. This is a 9 Month of endings; not the time to begin major new undertakings. While you allow the year to wind down naturally, you can share some of your management skills with a community organisation. A relationship that has served its purpose may come to an end. You may feel a little emotional, or uncertain as you prepare to move forward. Take a family vacation, bring your family to the beach, and get some much-needed rest.

Exercise 1. Preparing for Your 6 Personal Year

1. Relative to your Life Path, Birth Day number, and personal experience of the number 6, how do you feel about your responsibilities toward those who are close to you? Is there love, balance, peace, and harmony in your life?

2. Go back to the last time you experienced a 6 Personal Year. What was going on in your personal and professional life at that time? Were you at peace? Was there balance in your relationships? Were you able to receive the support you needed from others to accomplish your goals?

3. Relative to where you are in your life at this time, how would you like to see your relationships improved? For example, if you are a freedom-loving 5 Life Path, how could you be more

responsible? Or more balanced? If you are a deep-thinking and solitary 7 Life Path, consider how your solitary nature has affected your ability to build strong personal relationships. If you are a career-focused 8 Life Path, how can you bring more balance into your life?

4. Review your Key Life Sectors list. Are all these sectors still relevant at this time? If not, make any necessary changes or adjustments. Is there one area that needs more balance than others? Work on establishing balance between the various areas of your life.

5. Is there time in your hectic schedule for peaceful, healing, creative, or harmonious activities such as yoga, nature walks, the arts, or listening to music? Spending some time on an artistic project can have a very soothing effect on the soul. The key to a successful 6 Personal Year is to establish a sense of peaceful balance in your life, regardless of how crazy things may appear.

6. Put a little romance back into your life. This may be challenging, especially if you and your partner have grown apart over the past few years. Go out on dates where you pretend that you don't know each other. You may be surprised at how much you and your partner have changed. Become reacquainted. You could set your relationship on a whole new course.

7. If you tend to be over-involved in the affairs of others, how can you be more respectful of personal boundaries? Meddling can cause resentment. What do you fear you will lose if you pull away a bit and establish more healthy boundaries? Get counselling if this is a challenge for you.

Exercise 2: Year-End Review

1. In what ways did you bring more balance and harmony into your life?
2. What are the benefits from this increased balance?
3. What is the most important lesson you learned this year?
4. What new knowledge will you bring into your upcoming 7 Personal Year?

CHAPTER 10

The 7 Personal Year

Reflection, Analysis, the Inner Life

As a counterbalance to the pull of responsibilities and relationships of last year, the addition of a 1 to the 6 generates the unusual and sometimes challenging energy of the 7 Personal Year. You are now in the third and final phase of your 9-Year Epicycle. The 7 year brings a period of temporary withdrawal from the hustle and bustle of worldly and material existence. 7 is the number of the inner life. It requires that you get in touch with your innermost values and desires, which can put you at odds with the generally more materialistic standards of the world around you.

Your current epicycle has no doubt built up significant momentum by now, and you may be ready for a break. I like to call the 7 Year the "calm before the storm," except that *storm* carries such negative connotations. Maybe it could be called "The calm before the big hurrah!" It's a period of regrouping while you gather your inner strength and resources to be better prepared to go all out in your big 8 Personal Year coming next year. Although no one really likes to slow down, you may need this timeout to catch your breath and refocus on your goals.

One of the purposes of this period of reflection is to allow you the opportunity to fully digest and integrate the lessons acquired through your experiences to date. The better you understand yourself and the way you respond to life situations, the more likely you will be to make the most of your upcoming trends. This is a year of introspection, analysis, and seclusion. This is a good time for studies, especially if additional learning will give you the skill set you need to be in a better position to take advantage of rising opportunities.

This is the ideal time to take up an activity that requires a certain degree of quiet and solitude. Although you will continue to pursue your daily activities as before, you will have a greater need than usual for moments of seclusion. Take long, hot baths in the evening, set time aside to read or listen to inspirational works, get up early in the morning and go for long walks in the park, do a half-hour of yoga, tai chi, qigong, meditation, or deep-breathing exercises. Your best strategy now is to turn your focus inward. Running about and pursuing material goals will bring less satisfaction, lead to fewer results, and could also prove to be unhelpful.

In fact, in a 7 Personal Year, pursuing material goals alone can be counterproductive. Andrea, a hard-working 13/4 Life Path financial advisor, experienced an intense period of self-questioning during her 7 Personal Year. With several years of dedicated hard work behind her, she had reached a certain level of success in her position. However, she felt that she would not reach her full potential unless she made a career move. She pursued several avenues during that year, went on many job interviews, but nothing worked out. For Andrea, money was one of the major issues. There was never enough to justify a job change.

In September of that year, a 16/7 month of intense analysis and introspection, once again she was faced with a couple of career options. However, the position she really wanted fell short of her desired salary range. Since she was in a 16/7 month, I suggested she take money out of the equation and consider the job on its deeper merits. She gave it further thought, recognized that this was the best job given her talents and abilities and career goals, and decided to accept the position, despite the lower pay. To her surprise, the following day upper management reconsidered her salary demands, and she was given the amount

CHAPTER 10 • THE 7 PERSONAL YEAR

she had originally wanted. Sometimes it pays to follow your heart rather than the money.

Not to worry, this period of withdrawal from the material world is temporary. You have not suddenly become an antisocial recluse. It's just that you need a bit of timeout for yourself. Years of intensive focus on the outside, material world need to be balanced by introspection and non-material concerns. Re-evaluate your goals and long-term aspirations. Measure your progress. Ensure that your expectations for future accomplishments are realistic. After this year, only two years remain in the current epicycle. Learn to appreciate yourself, simply, as you are, not defined by the requirements of the outside world. Self-love is an invaluable asset.

A friend of mine, a successful author, counsellor, and businesswoman, a typical 8 Life Path woman, decided to plan a trip to El Camino for an upcoming 7 Personal Year. At first, I thought the idea sounded quite appropriate, a meditative, spiritual journey, quiet time spent in nature. Then the innate 8 Life Path energy kicked in (along with other 8s active at the time) and the project suddenly began to grow into a more impressive undertaking, including the writing of a journal for eventual publication. At that point, I started to think that although filled with incredible potential, the project seemed more appropriate for an 8 or even a 9 Personal Year. As it turned out, once the 7 Personal Year finally arrived, another opportunity arose, requiring a radical move and almost total seclusion to a small town in the country, a typical 7 environment. The El Camino adventure was postponed for another time.

It is not uncommon to experience feelings of specialness and superiority in a 7 period. A 7 Year can send certain individuals into a self-critical, overly analytical tailspin. The inward pull of the 7 energy can be difficult to handle, and you may struggle hard to keep from slipping into the clutches of negative thinking, loneliness, or even depression. Fighting against the natural trend toward introspection will only lead to feelings of frustration, confusion, and resentment.

A 7 Personal Year is typically not a year for manifesting great outward achievement. Progress generally remains below the surface, expressed more as a deepened understanding of self and of life. It may also manifest as a greater knowledge in your field of work or expertise. You will experience far more personal satisfaction at the end of the year if you have allowed yourself to develop a positive and healthy relationship with your inner life.

The 7 Personal Year Month by Month

JANUARY (8 Personal Month): Material Accomplishment, Career

As the 7 Personal Year is introspective in nature, this would be a good month to set up your agenda for the year in such a way as to give yourself more time for thought and reflection. Scheduling some personal time into your weekly agenda will be very beneficial. Focus on planning and goal setting for the next two or three years. This is a good month for career and business activities. You have great ideas that can be turned into innovative projects in business or at work. You are getting a good sense of which of your projects you will be able to bring to completion as the current epicycle approaches its peak next year. You are progressing with increased confidence and self-assurance now. Questions bearing on the meaning of life may start to pique your interest as you move forward toward achieving your goals.

FEBRUARY (9 Personal Month): Completion, Endings, Giving

Projects that need to be completed this month could keep you from the alone time you seek. You will need to be considerate of the feelings of others if you don't want to push people away. The stirrings of deep inner questioning may make you feel somewhat uncomfortable. You may wonder about the satisfaction you derive from your work, your relationships, or your lifestyle. After having built up a momentum over the past few years, working hard toward the accomplishment of your goals, you may find it disquieting to suddenly find yourself questioning all aspects of your life. You may feel overly emotional, easily irritated by the demands made by others. Release some of the activities or people that no longer serve a purpose in your life. Wait until next month before making important changes.

MARCH (1 Personal Month): Originality, Self-Determination

This month marks the start of a complete 9-month cycle, indicating the potential for much inner growth and progress throughout the year. This is an excellent time to begin studies, meditation, or quiet reflective practices such as tai chi, yoga, or even gardening and reading. If you have been putting off a research or study project for later, now is the time to begin. Proceed with confidence with a challenging new project, something that you can sink your teeth into, or something that will force you to think, analyze, and work out complex issues. A 1 Personal Month in a 7 Personal Year is a time in which you will be particularly self-focused. Be aware of a tendency to be overly selfish, lest you hurt the ones who matter to you.

APRIL (11/2 Personal Month): Sharing, Joint Projects, Intuition

You will probably be required to work closely with others this month, an experience that could cause you a bit of frustration, given that you are more inclined to do your own thing this year. This can be an intense month, during which you will be working hard at resolving complex problems but then not seeing immediate results. Patience in all areas, especially when working with others, is required. Your intuition is working overtime and you are motivated from deep within to pursue certain avenues of interest. Inner guidance is a strong force now and can provide you with valuable creative solutions to immediate problems. Remain focused on the task at hand. Interactions with another person could inspire a deeper understanding of yourself. Keep an open mind, and avoid making rash decisions.

MAY (3 Personal Month): Creativity, Self-Expression, Enjoyment

Although still in a reclusive year, you are inclined to socialize a bit this month, as you need a much-deserved break from all that introspection. Yet, even in your socializing you will be more interested in discussing serious topics than wasting time on superficial chitchat and idle gossip. The 7 Personal Year has begun to draw you deeper inside; you may be reflecting on the meaning of life, as well as your life purpose. You may find it difficult to pull yourself out of your inner musings and focus on the mundane. Be careful not to fall into excessive analysis and criticism this month. Focus on a quiet, enjoyable, creative task. You could enjoy journaling, participating in a book club or other discussion group. Use creative ways of exploring your inner self.

JUNE (13/4 Personal Month): Work, Focus, Dedication

As a means of returning to your seclusion, you won't mind being buried in hard work this month, especially if this work can be done alone. There is no way around it: you will have to attend to the details of day-to-day life, both at home and on the job. You could grow impatient with trivial matters and details this month. However, by keeping your nose to the grindstone, this could be a very productive month. A well-organized routine will make the days go by more smoothly. Work with your weekly planner and manage your time efficiently. Stick to the task at hand. You could enjoy spending some time on a home or garden project, or tweaking your recipe for your favourite cookies. You are focused on your interests now; remember to reach out to close ones; involve your spouse or children in a home project.

CHAPTER 10 · THE 7 PERSONAL YEAR

JULY (14/5 Personal Month): Surprises, Change, Expansion

This month brings a complete change of pace as the energy picks up considerably. While last month you needed to stick to your agenda, this month you will need to be more flexible. Keep an open mind; unexpected news or events could cause you to rethink some of your plans. You could be feeling restless, anxious to get on with some of the ideas you've been mulling over these past few months. Unforeseen circumstances could intrude on your alone time, but that's okay. You could use a little change and adventure in your life right about now. Remain flexible so as not to grow frustrated if your agenda gets shuffled around. Your mind is keen and you are eager to explore new areas of interest. Capable of thinking outside the box, you could find original solutions to long-standing problems. Focus on new or innovative approaches.

AUGUST (6 Personal Month): Family, Home Life, Balance

After last month's excitement, you will need to add a little balance in your routine. Even though you may be eager to return to doing your own thing, you will benefit greatly by spending time with family and close friends. Comfort and support received from others will do wonders for your restless soul. A special relationship could deepen as a result of time well spent together. A 6 Personal Month is always a time for balanced giving and receiving. Domestic and job responsibilities may be a priority this month. By choosing for peace and harmony, you will enjoy your time addressing problems and finding solutions. A family vacation to a quiet location would do you and your loved ones a world of good. Take some time out to listen to music, read, or enjoy your favourite hobby. Your creativity could flow smoothly this month.

SEPTEMBER (16/7 Personal Month): Analysis, Reflection, Isolation

This year you have spent much time in thought, and this month, you may feel the need to withdraw even more. Guard against the tendency to over-analyze and to be overly critical of yourself or of others. You question everything, but be patient, for answers must come in their own time. Much personal growth is possible if you allow the inner transformation to occur naturally. This is an intense time, with much learning and an increased sense of self-awareness. This is not the time to plan a family vacation or important social or public events. If you feel yourself growing depressive, go for long walks, spend some time in the garden, or get in touch with nature. Find a like-minded friend with whom to share your feelings and thoughts. Read an inspirational book.

OCTOBER (8 Personal Month): Business, Practical Awareness

You are now in a position to start applying much of what you have learned this year, whether about yourself, about life, or about your job or career. You are in no mood for superficialities, and you have a no-nonsense approach to business, work, and money matters this month. Excellent progress can be made in career and business now. You have grown stronger in self-knowledge and understanding, and you are in a better position to make decisions that reflect your true life purpose. This may cause you to rethink some of the goals you set for yourself several years ago. You are now preparing for an 8 Personal Year, during which you will have the opportunity to put it all together, finally accomplishing your goals. You could be feeling quite confident, and should definitely reward yourself for your efforts.

NOVEMBER (9 Personal Month): Completion, Release

This year's journey into the depths of your life experience has very likely brought you much self-knowledge. As the year comes to a close, this intense learning process is coming to an end. Soon you will begin to feel a deep relief. If you have attended to your inner life, you will have grown much. If you have resisted it and ignored its call, you could feel uncertain about your upcoming 8 Year. The 8 Personal Year is a year of harvest; as you have sown, so shall you reap. Your efforts of the past years will show concrete results. This can be frightening if you have ignored your duties and responsibilities to yourself and to others along the way. For the time being, let go, finish projects, and relax. Wait for the renewal of energy that the next month, a 1 Personal Month, will bring. Volunteer some time and energy with your preferred community organization. Focus on others rather than on self.

DECEMBER (1 Personal Month): Renewal, Initiative, Rebirth

Based on everything you have learned this year, you are probably ready to make a few changes in your life. You've done a lot of thinking, and you have greater self-awareness now. Your energy level is up, and you feel invigorated and prepared to tackle any challenges the world might put on your path. You may be sensing that your big year is coming, and it is. Your focus is very much on yourself now, so don't forget to balance your week with time out for family and friends. Avoid making hasty decisions; the time is not quite right yet. Keep in mind that you are approaching the end of the epicycle; any changes you implement now should contribute to bringing current projects to completion. Focus on short-term goals.

Exercise 1. Preparing for Your 7 Personal Year

1. Relative to your Life Path, Birth Day number, and personal experience of the number 7, evaluate your ability to spend quality time alone. Are you comfortable reflecting, meditating, and turning inward for guidance? Are you able to connect with inner guidance when in need of direction?

2. Recall the last time you experienced a 7 Personal Year. What was going on in your life at that time? Were you attempting to forge ahead toward outward and material accomplishments, or did you respect your need for quiet and contemplation?

3. Relative to where you are in your life at this time, how can you improve on your connection with your inner self?

4. Review your Key Life Sectors list. Are all these sectors still relevant? Schedule some quiet time in your daily agenda. Let others know that you need time for reflection. You don't have to be a recluse and alienate people in the process. Read inspirational books, listen to inspirational talks, and watch inspirational videos. Allow for some quiet time in nature.

5. Consider deepening your expertise, either personal or professional, through study, research, or courses. Is there an area of your life that would benefit from additional learning? A 7 Year is an excellent time to hone your skills or develop a unique expertise.

6. Are their social responsibilities that could be cut back to allow you more personal quiet time? This is not the best time to host a fundraising event! Focus on solitary activities.

7. Reflect on your overall situation, personally and professionally. Review the long-term goals you set for yourself six years ago, at the beginning of this epicycle. Have you progressed according to your plans in all sectors of your life? Have you overlooked anything important? Without being judgmental, measure your progress.

8. Keeping in mind that your current epicycle will be coming to an end in two years, i.e. at the end of the next 9 Personal Year, reflect on what you need to do to bring this cycle to a successful close. What projects need to be finished? What relationships need to be released? Or healed? A review of your situation will teach you valuable lessons in goal setting,

which you will be able to apply once the next epicycle begins. Overall, assess your progress. Did you set goals that were realistic and attainable? What would you do differently in the next cycle?

Exercise 2: Year-End Review

1. What benefits did you derive from your quiet times? In what ways have you grown?
2. How do you feel about your progress now? Are you content with your life?
3. What is the most important lesson you learned this year?
4. What new knowledge will you bring into your upcoming 8 Personal Year?

CHAPTER 11

The 8 Personal Year

Power, Accomplishment, Satisfaction

This is it! The big year, the peak of your epicycle. Naturally, the dedication and the work you put into achieving your goals will determine if this will be a rewarding or a disappointing year. Composed of two 4s, the 8 is about as solid as it gets. The 8 represents the ultimate in personal and worldly accomplishment. If you have made choices that honour your talents and abilities, as well as the trends of your personal cycles, you are likely feeling pleased for all your hard work.

The 8 is sometimes associated with the concept of karma, which is often perceived as a negative energy. Karma simply reflects the law of cause and effect. Some people fear the 8, but shouldn't, especially if they have been sincere in their efforts. This is the year in which you will reap the fruits of your hard work of the past seven years. If you worked hard, were aligned with your true life purpose, and applied the necessary efforts, then this year will bring success, accomplishment, and great satisfaction. If, on the other hand, you have lived your life without structure and purpose, floating along without direction, this year could be frustrating and discouraging, even filled with difficulty and additional stress. There really is no magic formula—hard work leads to results, the absence of work leads to failure and disappointment.

The 8 is the number of the paymaster, and it will reward you in direct proportion to the intention and effort you have expended.

The 8 Personal Year is an excellent time to go all out and reach for your goals, to make them concrete. It is also an excellent time for career, business, and financial activities. Now you can go for the position, the power, and the success. Rewards will equal the efforts you have made over the past several years. If, on the other hand, you have made unwise choices, the 8 Personal Year can spell financial challenges. Business failures and personal bankruptcies are not uncommon in the 8 Year.

This is the year in which your hard work will be rewarded. Recognition, promotions, bonuses, awards, and career advancement are favoured in the 8 Year, but along with these often comes added responsibility. Your leadership skills could be put to good use as you express your vision. You can make things happen now. You have the power, the authority, the skills and ability, as well as the experience to see things through to completion. You are the expert, the master, and the authority in your field, as well as in your life. If you have dreamed of improving your personal or professional life, now is the time to go for it. Take control of your life. Feel self-empowered. You've worked hard for it. Enjoy it!

Not all people respond to success in the same way. Amanda was a high-level Human Resources executive in the male-dominated aerospace industry. Up until the age of 38, like most women in her position, she hadn't given much thought to having a child. Then, to her surprise, in a 5 Personal Year (a year of sudden and unexpected change) she became pregnant and gave birth to a son. While on maternity leave, a 6 Personal Year (family responsibilities, balance) she discovered the joys of motherhood. In the 7 Personal Year (analysis and introspection) she gave much thought to her situation, re-evaluating what was really important in her life.

After much reflection, Amanda concluded that although she had a fabulous career with all the perks and power any woman could possibly want, motherhood also mattered. She had reached a point in her life where she didn't want to be devoting all of her time and energy to her career. Knowing that she wouldn't be able

CHAPTER 11 • THE 8 PERSONAL YEAR

to negotiate the hours and working conditions she needed in order to spend more time with her son, she did the one thing she thought would get their attention. At the start of her 8 Personal Year, (a year of self-empowerment, harvest, and reward) and at the peak of her career, a position that she originally began in a 1 Personal Year, she handed in her resignation.

Note that Amanda was highly qualified, experienced, and very hard working. With an abundance of 4 energy among her numbers, she was a highly valued, dedicated asset to her employer. To her surprise, her boss turned around and offered her carte blanche to design the job conditions that would best suit her needs, if only she would reconsider her decision to leave the company. This unexpected turn of events put her in the unique position of paving the way for the many other women who had postponed motherhood for fear of jeopardizing their careers. Together they could now work out a solution for the unique needs of women and motherhood. This project, clearly a number 8 expression, would have a far-reaching and much-needed impact on her corporate environment.

This example doesn't suggest that everyone with a job-related grievance should quit their job and expect to be offered the ideal work solution on a silver platter. What it does show is that if you do the work, when the time is right, the rewards and the recognition and the opportunities are usually there.

For some, the 8 Personal Year is a time for re-evaluating long-term career goals. If you made questionable choices at the beginning of the current epicycle and are not satisfied with your direction, you could be facing some important decisions now. The 8 is a year of reckoning. Many people make important career changes in the 8 Personal Year. However, if you should find yourself in this situation, keep in mind that you are at the end of a 9-Year Epicycle, and will not begin the next epicycle for another two years. This means that you will probably not have a complete picture of your future direction until the new cycle kicks in.

If you plan on taking a completely new direction now, be aware that important adjustments could be made once you begin your next epicycle. If you can, avoid making long-term commitments, such as signing leases or agreements that last longer than the time that remains in your current cycle. Leave the door open for change and new opportunities.

The best approach in the 8 Personal Year is to complete what you have begun over the past few years. Try to derive some satisfaction from immediate results, rather than setting out on a new long-term path. Work with what you have. When all is said and done, remember to reward yourself for your achievements, whether great or small. If you've thought things through, made appropriate decisions and acted on them, then you've completed the process and have done well. Your accomplishments will contribute to the foundation of the next segment of your journey.

The 8 Personal Year Month by Month

JANUARY (9 Personal Month): Closure, Endings, Release

This epicycle is soon coming to a close, and you are probably starting to feel a strong urge to bring projects to completion. This is a good month to get some projects out of the way, especially those that might prevent you from successfully achieving your goals this year. You had plenty of opportunity to give serious thought to your goals and direction last year; now you are in a better position to make choices that are in tune with your inner purpose. Relieve yourself of unnecessary clutter in all aspects of your life, and focus on your goals. If you have done the work, this year has the potential for great accomplishment. Although you could be feeling some uncertainty, avoid dwelling on fears or insecurities. Negative thinking will only drag you down. Wait until next month before embarking on new projects.

CHAPTER 11 • THE 8 PERSONAL YEAR

FEBRUARY (1 Personal Month): Renewal, Beginnings, Initiative

February marks the beginning of the final thrust toward attaining personal and professional goals in your current epicycle. Now is the time to step up to the plate and give it all you've got. Be bold, courageous, and assertive. Your ambitions may rise to an all-time high as you set out to conquer the world. This is the time to overcome your fears and to be decisive. Yet, in your enthusiasm to forge ahead with your plans, try not to be overly aggressive or selfish. Recall the balance learned in your 6 Personal Year. Begin new activities. Focus on your unique talents and abilities. Be creative and take initiative. If you are unable to overcome feelings of uncertainty, be patient with yourself, and don't force the issue. Things will fall into place very soon. Focus on accomplishment.

MARCH (11/2 Personal Month): Nervous Tension, Cooperation

Progress appears to slow down a bit this month. You will need to wait for the input of others before moving forward. Decisions are not entirely up to you at this time. Your heightened sensitivity and nervous tension could lead you to make impulsive moves. Wait for a day when you feel more balanced before making important decisions. Try to establish an environment of peace and harmony, in all aspects of your life. It is important that you remain open to the ideas of others, and refrain from making snap judgments. Keep your feelings to yourself; go for a walk, let the emotional tide fall before approaching others on matters that carry potential conflict. At work, you can inspire others to support you in your efforts. Use those antennas to gather any inner guidance you may need at this time.

APRIL (3 Personal Month): Opportunities, Joy, Recognition

April should be a great month in many ways, especially in terms of social, personal, and work interactions. You feel optimistic and lucky, as things seem to be going in the right direction for you. Colleagues and friends approach you with opportunities and a willingness to participate in activities with you. Try to delegate or postpone some of your more tedious tasks and responsibilities. You are more in the mood to party than to work. Be careful of a tendency to spend money on frivolous things this month. Since this is a 3 Month in an 8 Year, try to find ways of bringing joy and creativity into your work projects. Organize a company barbeque or social event, or even a fundraiser. Spend time with friends during your leisure hours. Take a break now, even take your annual vacation, as next month you will need to buckle down, and get serious with work.

MAY (13/4 Personal Month): Work, Details, Dedication

It's time to get back to work! If you are well organized by nature, you won't have any trouble getting back into the swing of things. If you aren't so well disciplined, you could find it rough going this month. By now, you realize the importance of focus and hard work in the achievement of your goals, but more importantly, you are now at the peak of your current 9-Year Epicycle. All of your efforts matter. Take care of details and address those challenging projects head-on. Try not to be overly rigid and inflexible; if something isn't working, go around it and take another approach. You won't get points for banging your head incessantly against the wall. Nor is this the time to slack off and give in to laziness. Lack of focus could cause you to fail to reach your goals. Your efforts will pay off later this year.

CHAPTER 11 • THE 8 PERSONAL YEAR

JUNE (14/5 Personal Month): Surprises, Change, Liberation

Take advantage of those new opportunities that will allow you to move closer to your goals. Since 8 is a power year, you may want to stretch yourself now, reach beyond your comfort zone, take some risks. Keep your agenda and your schedule loose this month; unexpected situations are likely to arise and you may need to adjust your plans a bit. This can be an exciting month, with great opportunities for growth and expansion. You are ready for change and adventure, so take a weekend or a few days off and dare to do something different. Have some fun, but remember to stay focused on your objectives for the year. Avoid excesses in all things. Try to be balanced, and don't fuss over details. You'll only become impatient. If possible, delegate, or set aside, the annoying aspects of your duties. You're not in the mood to be tied down right now.

JULY (6 Personal Month): Responsibility, Measure, Balance

This is an excellent month for career and money matters. You have been able to show what you can do, and your efforts will not go unnoticed. Growing feelings of empowerment extend to your personal life. You feel better equipped to make the changes that will bring increased harmony at home and at work. Although you are feeling on top of the world, this doesn't mean that you should allow yourself to be overbearing and pushy with those persons who are close to you. At this time it is important that you exercise moderation in all things. Intent on attaining your goals this year, you could grow resentful of demands made on you by someone close. Remind yourself of what is really important. Try to keep things balanced and in perspective. Schedule a relaxing weekend getaway with your partner or a good friend.

AUGUST (16/7 Personal Month): *Reflection, Analysis, Introspection*

It's time to take a close look at your accomplishments to date. The epicycle is soon coming to a close, and you need to measure your progress. This is not a good month for a family vacation, nor is it the best time for social events. You may feel inclined to isolate yourself a bit this month. Spend some quiet time reading, meditating, enjoying walks in nature, or working in your garden. You are very focused on your work and can handle complex issues. Your brain is working overtime as you try to come up with effective ways to address problems or make things run more smoothly. Keep in mind that your attitude has an impact on others. Also, avoid being overly critical of yourself if you have not attained your goals as planned. Simply readjust your goals to reflect your current reality as well as your accomplishments.

SEPTEMBER (8 Personal Month): *Power, Career, Accomplishment*

This is a power month, in a power year; a great month for using your skills and rising to the top of your profession. This is your time of accomplishment! Warn your family that you will be focusing on career more than on family and domestic issues. Obviously, this isn't the month for a family vacation. Be confident, authoritative, and dynamic this month, but remember that not everyone is running on your super-high level of energy. Be reasonable in your expectations. If you are impatient, impractical, or unrealistic, you could pay a heavy price for your lack of good judgment. Do not overextend yourself financially. Be patient, and make the most of what you now have. Change is coming soon; there will be plenty of opportunity to reconsider your options at a later date.

CHAPTER 11 • THE 8 PERSONAL YEAR

OCTOBER (9 Personal Month): Endings, Completion, Release

Finally, you are reaching the moment of completion. Bring those long-standing projects to a close. Be sensitive to the responses of others as activities reach their end. You could be feeling more emotional than usual, reluctant to release the old, hesitant or uncertain about what will be coming next. A business relationship could end now as you prepare to move on to other challenges. You may experience a sense of loss. Express kindness, compassion, and understanding in your interactions with others. Try to focus a bit on others, rather than just on yourself; donate some of your time to a charitable organization or community activity. Be generous. Let others benefit from your experience. Share your wisdom, rewards, and accomplishments.

NOVEMBER (19/1 Personal Month): Renewal, Energy, Beginnings

You may be sensing the start of a new year just around the corner and are eager for accomplishments and results. Feeling dynamic and energetic, you are ready to tackle whatever comes your way. You will need to balance enthusiasm with sensitivity. Forceful behaviour will not serve you well. Your current epicycle is coming to a close next year, after which a brand new period of your life will begin. However, some housecleaning is probably required before you can be free to move forward. There is no need to make rash decisions. You are feeling the confidence that is a natural consequence of your accomplishments of the past few years. This is an excellent month for all business or career matters. You could be inspired with new ideas or plans for the future. Again, take your time. You have a year of closure coming up, a 9 Personal Year.

DECEMBER (11/2 Personal Month): *Inner Growth, Intuition*

As this year of accomplishment winds down to a close, you may feel the need to pause, and reflect. You are particularly sensitive and responsive now, aware of your progress and growth. Tune into your intuition for insights, guidance, and inspiration for the coming 9 Personal Year, a time of release, completion, and endings. You may be feeling somewhat vulnerable, uncertain as to where the upcoming changes will lead you. This can be an emotional time. Don't let your idealism blind you to matters at hand. Try to remain practical. Not everyone sees things as you do. You may find it difficult to express your feelings. Look for creative outlets to release some of that pent-up emotional energy. Prepare to wind down, release, and let go.

Exercise 1: Preparing for Your 8 Personal Year

1. Relative to your Life Path, Birth Day number, and personal experience of the number 8, how do you feel about your accomplishments to date? Are you confident that you will be able to reach the goals you established for yourself seven years ago? If not, why not?

2. Recall the last time you experienced an 8 Personal Year. What was going on in your career and in your personal life at the time? Were you in a position of personal and professional fulfillment? If not, why not?

3. Relative to where you are in your life at this time, what do you feel you need to do to bring the current cycle to a successful close? Can you revise your goals so that you will reach a satisfactory level of accomplishment this year and next? It is far better to set realistic goals that you can reach than unrealistic goals that you will fail to meet.

4. Review your Key Life Sectors list. Are all these sectors still relevant at this time? Focus on power and accomplishment.

CHAPTER 11 · THE 8 PERSONAL YEAR

Make any necessary changes or adjustments to your areas of focus. Express yourself with confidence.

5. Consider the long-term goals you set for yourself many years ago, both personally and professionally. Do you wish to keep these same goals for the next cycle? Is there something else you feel you need to accomplish in your life?

6. If you are self-employed or in a position that normally does not lend itself well to recognition, and you are reaching your goals, prepare to reward yourself for your efforts. Celebrate your achievements. Invite your friends and have a big party.

Exercise 2: Year-End Review

1. In what areas did you accomplish your goals?

2. How do you feel about your progress now?

3. What is the most important lesson you learned this year?

4. What new knowledge will you bring into your upcoming 9 Personal Year, a year of completion and endings?

CHAPTER 12

The 9 Personal Year

Completion, Endings, Release

The 9 Personal Year wraps up the epicycle. It is a very important year in that it is the start of a major transition period and requires special attention and careful planning on your part. It is the end of a long cycle as well as a bridge to the next. It is a time of completion, a period of taking stock and winding down. As the current epicycle comes to a close, you will want to stand back, look at the big picture, consider where you have been, what you have accomplished, and begin to consider where you would like to go next. It is a time for releasing and healing any outstanding bumps and bruises you may have sustained on your journey to date. It is a period of integration; the time to digest and absorb the lessons and experiences you have acquired.

It is not uncommon to experience nervousness, some anxiety, and heightened emotions, or even a sense of disorientation or confusion in a 9 Personal Year. An unknown future lies just around the corner, not yet fully determined, while the past still weighs down on you. This is a time for having a universal outlook on life, for opening your mind to broader horizons. Many people experience an explosion of creativity in a 9 Personal Year, giving them lots of ideas for possible future projects. It is very easy to become completely distracted now, as old structures are released and new possibilities seem to jump up at every turn.

The 9 Year is a time for selflessness. The more you think of yourself, the more you are likely to grow confused or discouraged.

Turn your focus toward others now and then. Share your talents, your wisdom, and your experience. Volunteer with your favourite organization or a local community group. You have learned much in this epicycle. You will more easily internalize and integrate what you have learned by finding ways of sharing it with others.

This is the best time to clean house, both literally and metaphorically. De-clutter your life. Finish off or consider abandoning, or just setting aside, long-standing, outdated projects. Unload all unwanted or unnecessary clutter from your life, including people. In a word, release anything that might hold you back and weigh you down before moving forward. This is the best time to hold the garage sale of the decade!

What is no longer appropriate or needed now will likely work its way out of your life as new opportunities arrive on the horizon. The degree and nature of the housecleaning required in your 9 Personal Year will depend on where you are in your life journey. If you find that you have veered significantly off course, then this would be the time to consider releasing your hold on the reins of your wayward chariot. This may require that you abandon an unhealthy work environment, leave a failed relationship, partnership, or marriage, or even leave town.

On the other hand, if your life is relatively on track, and you are heading in a healthy direction on your Life Path, then perhaps only moderate or light housekeeping is required, like getting to that basement or garage you've been promising to clean out for what seems like forever. All forms of release will be beneficial, as it is an indicator to the unconscious mind that you are ready to let go of the old, and prepare for the new. Keep in mind that a full glass cannot be fully refilled until it has first been emptied.

If you fear letting go, you may find this period challenging. In the 9 Year, there is a definite sense of something new about to emerge. However, you are still in the old epicycle, the new cycle not yet having been clearly defined. You may be uncertain about your future direction, which may only come into focus

CHAPTER 12 · THE 9 PERSONAL YEAR

later in the year, or early in the next, the 1 Personal Year, when you experience a rebirth of energy and vision.

The 9 Personal Year is like the garden in winter, flattened and hidden beneath the snow, dormant, not visible. Not until spring do the grass and the flowers rise up again and come to life. Our experience of this transition from one cycle to the next is similar, with our vision and energy diminishing somewhat in the 9 Year only to be reborn in the 1 Personal Year when, rejuvenated and renewed, we see clearly once again the path that lies before us.

It is important to be patient in the 9 Year, and especially to get plenty of rest. Self-care should be at the top of your list this year. Since energy levels tend to diminish during this year, there appears to be a higher incidence of illness and health issues, especially for people over the age of 40. In northern latitudes where winters are harsh and flu viruses abound, the 9 Personal Year can prove to be challenging to the immune system, especially in the fall and early winter months.

In an ideal world, everyone would be allowed to take a year off, or at least a fair part of it, at the end of the 9-Year Epicycle. Since we don't live in an ideal world, at least not yet, we need to create a lifestyle that favours our own health and well-being. If you are not in a position to take a sabbatical from your work, you may consider negotiating a four-day or five-day workweek. If that isn't possible, try an extra long vacation, especially during the second half of the year. This year, plan for some time off, rest, meditate, study, travel, or maybe just do nothing! With a little planning—okay, with some efficient long-term financial planning—you can squirrel away enough money for an extended vacation in your next 9 Personal Year.

Many people suffer burnouts or illness in a 9 Personal Year because they refuse to slow down. Face it, the pace of life hasn't gotten any slower in the past fifty years, and since we've seemingly accepted and adjusted to this speeding up of life, it's not likely to slow down anytime soon. And if you want to stay in business, keep your job, hold your family together, and reach your goals, it's in your best interests to keep up with the pace. Valiant efforts at keeping pace notwithstanding, eventually your mental, physical, or emotional body could suffer the brunt of this unnatural acceleration. That is why this point cannot be stressed enough: in a 9 Personal Year slow down, downsize, unload, relax, and above all, get some rest. Schedule a spa day once a month, take up yoga, tai chi, qigong, go for massages, meditate, relax, listen to soothing music, breathe, go for quiet drives in the countryside, or take long walks in the park.

As this is a year of endings, keep in mind that anything begun in a 9 Year may not be carried through into your next year. For that reason, it is not wise to start important new projects, make major career moves, begin a business, or start a course of study until the next cycle begins. The 9 Year contains energy from an old cycle that is coming to a close. There is usually insufficient energy to sustain an important new endeavour for a long period of time. This applies also to relationships; many relationships begun in a 9 Year do not last very long.

In the winter of a 9 Year, Caroline, a Life Path 8, was finishing the last semester of her college studies. She decided to split that last semester in two, which required stepping down from the honours program. However, this gave her more time to spend with friends and to play rugby. That fall, she completed her college studies, and then applied for the university program she was aiming for. The following January, the start of a brand new 9-Year Epicycle, she started on her journey. By the end of that epicycle, she had received a Bachelor of Science, a Masters Degree and a PhD in her field. You can't beat the charge and power of that number 8!

Betty, a 4 Life Path with strong family values, was married in a 9 Personal Year and divorced twenty-seven years later, three complete epicycles later. Although the marriage lasted a long time, a very long time by today's standards, not long into the 1 Personal Year, just after getting married, she realized that she had made a serious mistake. In those days, divorce was rarely

CHAPTER 12 • THE 9 PERSONAL YEAR

an option and marriage was taken very seriously. Initially, Betty was determined to make it work. Then, children came. Following her 4 Life Path, she did what she had to do to ensure the wellness of her family. In the end though, no amount of adjusting or bending could make her spend her entire life in an abusive relationship. Once relieved of her child-rearing duties and well established in a business of her own, in a 9 Personal Year, she finally left the marriage.

Sometimes, people will respond to this call for release by making strange choices. I have seen some go off on radical tangents in a 9 Year, only to realize a couple of years later, the error of their decision. Many of these wayward decisions are made under the mistaken assumption that anything new is better than the old. Tired of the old, people look for something new. However, given that the new cycle has not yet kicked in, it is best that you try cutting your hours, or exploring new opportunities on the side, before quitting your day job. Once the new year rolls around, you will have a better perspective on things, and may even come to the conclusion that what you had wasn't so bad after all, or that maybe it just needed some minor adjustments.

Carmen, a 9 Life Path with a 9 Birth Day, was a self-employed professional translator specialized in the field of ISO Standards. This was a very challenging job, which, over time, can lead to extreme mental fatigue. She had been operating a very successful business from her home for fifteen years when she reached a 9 Personal Year. She had lived in the Orient for a while, and had done some travelling over the years, experiences that she had very much enjoyed, which reflected the significant 9 energy in her numbers.

At the peak of her epicycle, with a successful business supporting a comfortable lifestyle, she reached a point of saturation in her career. She was tired, and began to grow increasingly bored with the work, a new sentiment, since for most of the previous years, she had enjoyed the challenges of the technical fields she encountered in her profession. She needed a new interest. This is when her enjoyment of travel suddenly flourished into a new passion.

In the 8 Personal Year, ready to take on new challenges, she began a course of studies in the travel industry. In the following 9 Personal Year, eager to expand her horizons and by then very tired of her translation work, she jumped on an opportunity to work for a travel-related business. At first, she found it exciting to go to work outside the home. Learning new job skills gave her a well-needed renewal of energy. But the charm of the new adventure soon wore off; a desk job was definitely going to be boring. By the fall of that 9 year, she concluded that over the years, her home-based translation business had afforded her a very good lifestyle, a level of freedom and autonomy she very much needed and enjoyed, and validation for being very successful in an intellectually and mentally challenging field. This lifestyle had also allowed her to be present for her daughter while she was growing up. All in all, she concluded, she had a pretty good deal. In the following 1 Personal Year, Carmen renewed her commitment to her business. To fulfill her need for change, she engaged in major renovations in her home, updating the living spaces to better suit her needs and those of her college-age daughter.

At the end of a 9 Personal Year, Josh, an R&D tax consultant with degrees in economics and taxation decided to sign up for a three-year cabinet-making course. He had always wanted to know how to work with wood. Needless to say, once in his 1 Personal Year, his vision cleared up. He left this program and enrolled at university to further his education in a field that was more closely related to his R&D work. A minor distraction along the way, the cabinet-making course did give him the skills to build a deck in his backyard.

In a 9 Personal Year, focus on finishing off projects, get rid of clutter, and slow down. It's fine to open doors and explore new options, however, it's best to not make binding long-term commitments. Consider postponing the signing of leases or contracts until the new year. Try temporary approaches. If you are looking for a new line of work, take a part-time or temporary job in that field. Close the doors to what is outdated. Open doors on the new without making final decisions.

The 9 Personal Year Month by Month

JANUARY (1 Personal Month): Autonomy, Self-Focus, Action

Now is the time to take the first steps in reviewing all aspects of your life, from personal to professional. Focus on yourself as you begin the last leg of your long, nine-year journey. Although you may experience growth and progress in your work this month, you could be starting to wonder if this is the direction you wish to pursue in the long run. This is the beginning of the end, and you may be feeling a little anxious to make changes in your life. However, the path you are to follow in the future has probably not yet made itself clear. Take action now, push forward with projects, make some changes, as this is a 1 Personal Month, but be patient, insofar as the larger, long-term changes are concerned. It's not unusual to feel a bit lost or confused now. You are just at the beginning of an important transition period.

FEBRUARY (11/2 Personal Month): Intuition, Inner Guidance

Projects could be moving at a slower pace right now. You may be questioning some of the decisions you made last month. Be receptive, and especially, be patient. Trying to change things too quickly will only result in frustration or confusion. Be alert to your heightened intuition. You are particularly sensitive to inspiration, and could be guided from within as to which steps to take in moving away from your old cycle into your new one next year. There is no need to be overly dramatic. It's not the end of the world, only the end of an epicycle. You feel particularly vulnerable and sensitive in personal relationships, and can take things personally. Try not to take yourself or your situation too seriously. Seek out the support of someone you trust, someone who can be there for you.

MARCH (3 Personal Month): Sociability, Creativity, Optimism

You may enjoy social events this month or time spent with friends. Entertain and be entertained. You probably could use a little fun time out, as the 9 Personal Year often proves to be emotionally draining. Complete activities or projects you started with friends. Use creative means to finish old projects. You are feeling more optimistic about the future, and can begin to think of your new life direction. However, this is not the time to commit to ideas that might involve long-term decisions, no matter how exciting they may seem. This is a great month for a vacation. You feel more like relaxing or playing than working. Even though a romantic encounter is possible, remember that this is a year of endings. Take your time. Wait until next year to make a serious commitment.

APRIL (13/4 Personal Month): Work, Details, Order

Work is your priority this month, so don't plan a vacation for April. You could experience frustration as you struggle with your daily tasks while seeking to release yourself from past and present limitations. This can be a confusing time. It is probably becoming clearer to you now that things are coming to an end, as they should in a 9 Personal Year. Keep in mind that endings make way for renewal, rebirth, and new beginnings, which is what you will experience next year. Even though you are swamped with work, don't neglect your health. Fatigue could cause you to opt for fast foods or forgo regular exercise. Remain flexible as you work hard to bring projects to a close. Your dedication and persistence will bring progress in work, or home and favourite passion projects.

CHAPTER 12 · THE 9 PERSONAL YEAR

MAY (14/5 Personal Month): Instability, Change, Impatience

You could be frustrated as you are pulled between a need to finish old projects and a desire to move forward. You are feeling a growing desire for change and for freedom, but you may not yet have a clear picture of your future path. Take things slowly. Consider new options as they present themselves, without making any long-term commitments. This is a time of deep inner change and transformation. Try something new, but don't throw out the baby with the bath water. Your options will become clearer as the year comes to a close and you move into your new 9-Year Epicycle. Avoid impulsive, irrational decisions. Learn from past experience. Allow things to come to an end before beginning something new.

JUNE (6 Personal Month): Responsibility, Balance, Healing

This month brings a need for more balance, calm, and peace into your life. You enjoy time spent at home, with family. This is a good month for a peaceful vacation. Sort out your feelings, especially with regard to personal relationships. Are there issues that need to be looked at, old patterns that need to be released? Are your responsibilities toward others still valid now? This is a time for balance and for healing. If needed, get some counselling or coaching. Although you may be feeling a bit lost, take the time to share your recent experiences with loved ones. They will appreciate the confidence you place in them during your time of confusion. Next month you will want to spend some time alone.

JULY (16/7 Personal Month): Reflection, Solitude, Analysis

You may feel the need to take some time for yourself this month, time to consider all those matters that have been simmering and bubbling to the surface. This is not the best time to focus on money, business, or material concerns. Answers or solutions to these issues are more likely to emerge next month, and then next year. Consider the ending of the current epicycle, the goals you had set for yourself, and your actual accomplishments. Steer clear of a tendency to be self-critical, negative, or gloomy. Look inward with the intention of learning and gaining a deeper understanding of yourself and of others. Look for clues as to any changes you might need to make over the next several months to facilitate your transition into your next epicycle. Transition periods can require a bit of extra attention.

AUGUST (8 Personal Month): Finances, Career, Accomplishment

Business and career pick up momentum this month as projects move forward toward completion. You are feeling energetic and are focused on accomplishing your goals now. You may want to take a close look at financial matters this month, assess your income, debts, savings, or retirement portfolio. Concentrate on clearing out old debts and material obligations; avoid adding to your existing load. Remember that the more outdated baggage you can release now, the easier it will be to pursue a new direction in the upcoming new epicycle. To ensure your success in a business matter, consider the situation from the perspective of the other person. Your dedication and diligence pay off and you could be richly rewarded for your efforts. Although you may be experiencing a high level of personal satisfaction, it is not yet time to make concrete decisions for the future.

SEPTEMBER (9 Personal Month): Release, Completion, Endings

A 9 Personal Month in a 9 Personal Year can generate considerable emotional turmoil. You know that change is inevitable, but the time of rebirth is not yet here. Finish off projects, clear up loose ends, rid your life of meaningless clutter. Invite some friends and have a gigantic garage sale! Be generous. Donate unused goods to a local thrift shop or donation centre. This month could mark the end of a long-standing relationship or job situation. Your emotions run high, and you feel more vulnerable than usual. This can be a time of instability and uncertainty. Although you may be feeling anxious about moving forward, avoid making long-term commitments now, whether in personal relationships or for career or business. Focus on release and completion. And, above all, get some rest!

OCTOBER (1 Personal Month): *Renewal of Energy*

October brings a much-needed renewal of energy after a long year of endings and uncertainty. You will be able to phase out the completion of old projects and begin considering your options for the next epicycle. This transition will occur gradually, over the next four to six months, so there is no need to jump ahead of yourself. You could be meeting new people now as you begin to explore possibilities for the future. Be ready to replace old ways of doing things with new; old relationships with new; old ways of looking at life with a new outlook. Look within for guidance and follow your heart now, but don't rush into a long-term commitment yet. Think it through first. Soon, there will be plenty of opportunities for decision making.

NOVEMBER (2 Personal Month): *Pause and Reflection*

Take time out to reflect on your new direction, leaving any unanswered questions for the time being. Wait for feedback, be receptive, and especially, be flexible. You can't do it all in one day. Your 9 Personal Year hasn't quite come to an end yet. Progress may appear slow now. Spend quality time with a close friend; nurture your valued relationships. Seek the counsel of a trusted mentor on those matters that trouble you most. A budding new relationship could be growing deeper this month. Give yourselves the time to get to know each other well before making any decisions. You are feeling vulnerable and emotional. Find some quiet time. Let the dust settle.

DECEMBER (3 Personal Month): Enjoyment, Relaxation, Friendship

The year and the epicycle are coming to a close, finally! You will be in the mood to celebrate and share good times with friends and family. Have fun, party, take a vacation, travel, and enjoy yourself. You've been through a gruelling year, and most likely, a life-altering epicycle! Your optimism level is on the rise as you sense the arrival of a new cycle just around the corner. You are able to express yourself with flair and originality. Don't by shy; put your creativity to good use. Good news is coming. Take your time with new projects; relax a bit. You've earned your time out. There is no need to rush into things. You will have plenty of opportunity to set plans in motion throughout the next year and into the next epicycle.

Exercise 1. Planning your 9 Personal Year

1. Relative to your Life Path, Birth Day number, and personal experience of the number 9, do you feel ready to bring your projects to a close this year? Have you made plans and provisions for taking extra time off? Have you scheduled an extended vacation? How will you get extra rest?

2. Go back to the last time you experienced a 9 Personal Year. Did you experience fatigue? Did you have health issues? Did you feel the satisfaction and relief of endings and release, or grief and sorrow at having to part with difficult situations?

3. Relative to where you are in your life at this time, what situations, activities, and relationships need to be ended now?

4. Review your Key Life Sectors list. There may be some sectors that are no longer relevant. Consider the probability that

these will be modified or changed in the next epicycle. Prepare to release the old and make room for the new.

5. This year is really housecleaning time, in all ways. Make a list of unfinished projects. Prepare to discard baggage, feng shui your home—in fact, de-clutter all aspects of your life, literally and metaphorically. Let go, release, and forgive.

6. Look for any outdated habits you may be holding on to. Explore all facets of your life: health, work, day-to-day activities, relationships. Ask yourself: Why am I holding on to these habits? What benefit do they serve in my life at this time? What would happen if I abandoned these behaviours now? How would my life be different? How would it be worse? How would it be better? What good habit(s) could I develop instead?

7. In what ways can you give back to your community? Plan on volunteering, sharing your talents and abilities with a local organization.

Exercise 2: Year-End Review

1. In what areas did you experience completion and release?

2. How do you feel about your accomplishments now?

3. What is the most important lesson you learned this year?

4. What new knowledge will you bring into your upcoming 1 Personal Year, a year of new beginnings?

CHAPTER 13

The Pinnacle Numbers

If you're one of those people who consider themselves to be numerically challenged and you've gotten this far in the book, you're probably starting to really enjoy numbers by now. Maybe we can add one more number to our list? Are you ready for a bit more math? Or shall we say, easy math?

In astrological symbolism, mathematics is associated with the cardinal signs Aries and Libra (*Astrological Crosses: Exploring the Cardinal, Fixed & Mutable Modes*) and in particular with the planet Saturn. Saturn, interestingly, is also associated with authority figures and, in particular, the father. I have noticed that many of the people who have trouble with numbers also have experienced poor relationships with their father or with an authority figure. Sometimes the father was loving and caring, but he was simply absent, busy with job or career.

I developed an early love of numbers and mathematics because it was the easiest way to establish common ground with my dad, a brilliant electrical engineer. The infinite patience of his 9 Life Path tamed the restlessness and anxiety of my 14/5 Life Path. Throughout the difficult years of high school, no other subject had the appeal of algebra and geometry. Math was straightforward, clean, and direct, but mostly, it was refreshingly logical. There was never any ambiguity with numbers, as there was with ideas, beliefs, perspectives, relationships, and the shifting values of the sixties. With math, there was always one answer, the right answer, even if it was a zero. Opinions, feelings, preferences, beliefs, or impressions didn't matter.

Math was like solving puzzles. I'd stay up late at night just to attempt the level 3 problems, the advanced problems that were designed to really challenge our learning. If I couldn't figure out the answer, I'd go to sleep and, almost without fail, my brain would work out the problem during the night. I'd wake up the next morning and complete the equation. It was rewarding and validating. Here was something I could do right. Where everything else seemed confusing and often frightening, numbers never failed to come through. Mathematics was an oasis of order and logic in a world of chaos and uncertainty.

Another thing about numbers is that they don't lie. If your bathroom scale says that you weigh 185 pounds, there aren't many ways of interpreting your weight. If your bank account says that you're overdrawn by $6000, well, there aren't too many poetic ways of expressing that you're in the red. If you're in a 4 Personal Year, there's no getting around it, you'll have to face work, family, and home responsibilities. If you're in a 9 Personal Year, you'll have to let things go.

Now that you are familiar with the 9-Year Epicycle, you are most likely beginning to experience a greater sense of order, purpose, and direction. So far, we've been working with short- and medium-term cycles: Personal Days, Months, and Years. In this chapter, we'll introduce the Pinnacle numbers, which cover longer periods. These numbers act as a backdrop to the Life Path and Personal Year numbers and further refine the portrait of your journey, adding valuable information, not not only for planning and goal setting, but also for understanding your journey. With the addition of the Pinnacles, you'll be able to put together a more complete personal roadmap.

The Pinnacle Numbers

The Pinnacle numbers describe four periods along the journey, each with its own unique lessons and opportunities. They provide you with opportunities that your Life Path number may not offer you. For example, if you have a 4 Life Path, you may become entrenched in habits and old ways of doing things. A 5 Pinnacle will force you to be innovative and to break up the routine.

A Pinnacle change can indicate a significant seasonal change in your life, bringing a new set of experiences, challenges, and potential for learning. Look to Pinnacle changes to help you understand why you are attracted to certain types of experiences. Pinnacle numbers will also describe the nature of the situations you are likely to encounter during a certain period.

When setting long-term goals, consider the energy indicated by your current and upcoming Pinnacles. If you are about to begin a 6 Pinnacle, for example, you can expect increased responsibilities and a greater need for balance both at home and at work. Given that the trend is toward management positions and service to others, this might not be the best time to go live in a cave in Tibet. Look to Pinnacle changes for important information about changing tides and new opportunities.

Calculating the Pinnacle Numbers

The First Pinnacle covers the vital formative years of the life and should be studied closely when raising children, or when considering your own motivations and early conditioning. It is found by adding the numbers of the Month and Day of birth, and reducing to a single digit. The Second Pinnacle number is arrived at by adding the Day and Year of birth, and reducing to a single digit. The Third Pinnacle is equal to the sum of the First and Second Pinnacle numbers, while the Fourth Pinnacle is determined by adding the numbers for the Month and Year of birth. Remember to reduce the numbers to single digits, except for 11 or 22.

Pinnacle 1	Month + Day
Pinnacle 2	Day + Year
Pinnacle 3	Pinnacle 1 + Pinnacle 2
Pinnacle 4	Month + Year

Example calculations for a person born on June 29, 1971.

- Reduce the Birth Month number to a single digit or Master number: June = 6.
- Reduce the Birth Day number to a single digit or Master number: 29 = 2 + 9 = 11.
- Reduce the Birth Year number to a single digit or Master number: 1971 = 1 + 9 + 7 + 1 = 18, reduce again, 1 + 8 = 9.
- First Pinnacle number: Month plus Day, 6 + 11 = 17, reduce to single digit, 1 + 7 = 8.
- Second Pinnacle number: Day plus Year, 11 + 9 = 20, reduce to single digit, 2 + 0 = 2.
- Third Pinnacle number: First Pinnacle number plus Second Pinnacle number, 8 + 2 = 10, reduce to single digit, 1 + 0 = 1.
- Fourth Pinnacle number: Month plus Year, 6 + 9 = 15, reduce to single digit, 1 + 5 = 6.

Duration of the Pinnacles

To calculate the duration of the First Pinnacle, subtract the Life Path number from 36. In the example above, the Life Path for a Birth Date of June 29, 1971 is 8 (6 + 11 + 9 = 26; 2 + 6 = 8). With a Life Path 8, the First Pinnacle would last from birth until the end of the year in which the person turned 28 (36 − 8). The Second Pinnacle would begin in January of the following year, the year in which the person would turn 29. The Third Pinnacle would start in the year the person turns 38, and the Fourth Pinnacle would begin the year the person turns 47. Note that Pinnacles start in January of a 1 Personal Year, and finish at the end of a 9 Personal Year.

Pinnacle 1	36 - Life Path
Pinnacle 2	9 years
Pinnacle 3	9 years
Pinnacle 4	To end of life

CHAPTER 13 • THE PINNACLE NUMBERS

Duration of the Pinnacles				
Life Path number	First Pinnacle	Second Pinnacle	Third Pinnacle	Fourth Pinnacle
1	0-35	36-44	45-53	54 →
2/11	0-34	35-43	44-52	53 →
3	0-33	34-42	43-51	52 →
4/22	0-32	33-41	42-50	51 →
5	0-31	32-40	41-49	50 →
6	0-30	31-39	40-48	49 →
7	0-29	30-38	39-47	48 →
8	0-28	29-37	38-46	47 →
9	0-27	28-36	37-45	46 →

Working with the Pinnacles

Having worked through the calculations and exercises in the previous chapters, you are no doubt now quite familiar with the meaning of each of the Basic, Master, and High Energy numbers. Use your newly developed knowledge of the numbers to include your Pinnacles and make the best plans for your journey.

When evaluating an upcoming Pinnacle, first consider your experience with the numbers. If, for example, you generally lack courage, energy, and initiative, and are often fearful and dependent on others, you could be lacking in 1 energy. During a 1 Pinnacle you are likely to encounter situations that will challenge you to develop and use the positive traits of the 1, such as confidence, originality, and self-reliance. A 5 Pinnacle will bring opportunities for change, freedom, and new experiences, and will require flexibility and open-mindedness on your part. You can prepare for an upcoming Pinnacle change by becoming familiar with the energies of its corresponding number.

Also note if there are any High Energy influences behind the Pinnacle numbers. These can add an element of challenge to the period. A 19/1 Pinnacle might show a tendency to be overly wilful, too centred on the self. This can result in conflict when dealing with others. A 13/4 Pinnacle may be experienced as being overly restrictive. A 14/5 Pinnacle can bring much adventure and change, maybe too much! A 16/7 may indicate a need for isolation, triggering trouble in relationships, or difficulty fitting in. As in all cases where High Energy numbers are found, the degree of difficulty will be greatly attenuated, and eventually transmuted to the positive expression of the Basic number, as the individual, through continued growth and self-awareness, corrects the corresponding behaviours or attitudes.

The First Pinnacle can reflect limitations as well as opportunities, depending on your natural inclinations as indicated by the Life Path and Birth Day numbers. For a 5 Life Path person, for example, the discipline and order required during a 4 First Pinnacle can be challenging. Feelings of limitation and frustration may be even more strongly felt if the First Pinnacle is a 13/4 or if the Life Path is a 14/5. At the heart of the 5 Life Path is a deep desire for freedom. Although this person may resent the apparent limitations and rigour of the 4 Pinnacle, given a healthy and supportive environment, they may learn to work hard and perhaps develop the discipline and respect for order and perseverance that the 5 Life Path alone would not have offered. This particular combination, a 13/4 Pinnacle with a 14/5 Life Path and Birth Day, pushed me into a difficult Dark Night of the Soul period in my late teens, a deep and powerful learning phase of my life.

The Second and Third Pinnacles, lasting 9 years each, cover a large part of the middle life, touching the thirties and forties. They reflect the nature of those busy years of adulthood. An 8 in these Pinnacles is often very productive, offering significant opportunities for career advancement and financial growth. A 2 Pinnacle reflects a period in which relationships are highlighted, whether personal or professional, and is often a time for love and marriage, while a 6 Pinnacle can bring rewarding relationships, a busy family life, and opportunities to develop and use management skills.

The Fourth Pinnacle reflects the nature of the latter phase of life, including the retirement years. For many, this is an important period of integration. Some people will question the meaning and purpose of their lives now, looking for the value of their contribution to family, friends, or community. They re-evaluate their career or job. Many will make significant adjustments at this time, seeking to better reflect changed values and accrued learning. Freed of the responsibility of raising a family and building a career, it's not unusual for people to embrace this period as a time of profound inner transformation, healing, and growth.

As they approached their Fourth Pinnacles, many of my clients expressed interests that were quite different from their lifelong day jobs, for example, transitioning from computer programming to photography, or from graphic design to managing community projects. I have noticed that when the Fourth Pinnacle is very different from the previous three Pinnacles as well as the Life Path and Birth Day numbers, it can take the first 9-Year Epicycle to become accustomed to the new energy. In such a case, simply take the time needed to adjust to the new Pinnacle.

Examine this Pinnacle when setting long-term goals. If you have a number 4 Fourth Pinnacle, you may want to make sure that you have a hobby to fall back on when you retire. With 4 energy, you'll want to keep busy, work from home, or even renovate your home. If you have a 6 or a 9 among your numbers, you may want to help others organise their homes. If you have a 5 or a 9 Fourth Pinnacle, you may want to travel, explore the world, or express your unique life learning. A 7 Fourth Pinnacle will be indicative of a more reflective, quiet time of life, perhaps with a desire to find deeper answers about the nature of life, while a number 3 Fourth Pinnacle will likely offer plenty of opportunities to enjoy the social life, or to express yourself creatively.

The Pinnacle numbers also show why one person appears to have made sudden radical changes throughout their life, while another appears to have had a much smoother ride. Sometimes, these numbers are very similar in energy. For example, someone with a 6, 4, 2, and 6 series of Pinnacles has a pretty consistent pattern of working with people, or being in management or service-related jobs. On the other hand, someone with a 4, 14/5, 16/7, and 3 series of Pinnacles is likely to make some unexpected turns on their journey, as these numbers carry very different signatures. When considering the Pinnacles in the context of the Life Path, sometimes these radical changes can make sense. Perhaps certain important lessons needed to be learned before you could reach your full potential. When looking at your Pinnacles, remember to place them in the context of your Life Path.

As she reached the peak of her third pinnacle, a busy 14/5 with a wide range of experiences, Audrey, with a Life Path 1, decided to go all in and obtain her MBA. She was then ready to transition into her fourth pinnacle, a balanced, responsible 6, with an MBA in Change (5) Management (6)! Those numbers don't lie!

1 Pinnacle

This is a great time to express independence, courage, initiative, energy, determination, boldness, and enterprise. Focus on your personal goals, interests, and talents. It can be a period of rather intense self-discovery and should be used to develop your unique talents and abilities. You may find that you are pretty much on your own, and must proceed with little support from others. You will need to rely on yourself. Depending on your degree of self-confidence, this period can either be very productive, or very difficult. If you are insecure and in need of support from others, you could find the 1 Pinnacle rather challenging, especially if circumstances push you to be self-reliant. You have the opportunity now to create a new path forward, to develop original approaches in your field of expertise, or to branch out on your own. Use your leadership, originality, creativity, and organizational skills for your good and for the good of all.

2 Pinnacle

Relationships are usually very important during a 2 Pinnacle, and marriages are frequent at this time. This is not the time to think of yourself alone. Your sensitivity to the influences and needs of others is heightened, especially if this is an 11/2 Pinnacle. Your sensitivity could also extend to nature and the arts. You need a peaceful and quiet environment. You could be attracted to a helping profession such as counselling, coaching, a health-related field, or teaching. People are drawn to your charm, magnetism, and kindness. If you are a self-motivated and very independent person, you could find this period a bit challenging, as you will be required to pay some attention to the needs and demands of others. In a 2 Pinnacle, usually you are not alone. You may need to make adjustments to your lifestyle as you bring a spouse, partner, or children into your life. If you are in a troubled relationship, you could be faced with a divorce. Counselling, coaching, or mentoring could be very beneficial at this time. This Pinnacle requires that you be trustworthy, gracious, receptive, tolerant, diplomatic, considerate, and cooperative.

3 Pinnacle

The 3 Pinnacle can be a fun and enjoyable period. You will encounter plenty of opportunities for socializing, romance and for having a good time. In all areas, you should be positive and optimistic. If you feel yourself falling into negativity and moodiness, get help. The 3 can bring luck and fortunate opportunities and encounters. Tremendous creativity and imagination may be unleashed, and if you are an artist, you could get the lucky break that launches your career. This is an excellent time to expand your social network. There is often a strong need for self-expression, either verbally or through an artistic medium. Emotions can run high as sensitivity is heightened.

It is easy to become scattered, distracted, and disorganized in a 3 Pinnacle. You will need to remain focused so as not to lose track of your long-term goals. Oh, and it might be a good idea to make a budget!

4 Pinnacle

A 4 Pinnacle usually requires that you tend to the basics: job, home, health, fitness, and family issues. It is a period of slow growth that requires persistence, consistent effort, focus, structure, dedication, and perseverance. For some, it can be quite challenging, as limitations on time, money, and opportunity may be experienced. If this is a 13/4 Pinnacle, you could feel particularly frustrated. Courage and a positive attitude will need to be consciously maintained. You must focus on details and essentials. Order, organization, and method are required. Be patient and, especially, be realistic with your goals and expectations. Avoid becoming overly rigid. Home and property renovations or purchases are likely. Prepare for the future. Build a solid foundation now. Family obligations can take up a fair amount of your time. This can be a very productive time, especially if you are building a business or career. A 22/4 Pinnacle is demanding, but can lead to remarkable progress and financial rewards, especially if you are willing to work hard to build something of significance. You are the Master Builder now!

5 Pinnacle

A 5 Pinnacle can bring much movement, change, and varied experiences. It favours experimentation! This is an excellent period for expressing yourself different ways. There may be little in the way of stability in a 5 Pinnacle. When experienced early in life, this usually indicates some uncertainty and many changes in the family environment. A broad education can be helpful. There is a tendency during a 5 Pinnacle, especially a 14/5 Pinnacle, to make impulsive or risky decisions. If, in your previous Pinnacle, you felt burdened by limitations and responsibilities, you may want to break free now. Beware of a tendency for exaggeration, unrealistic expectations, impatience, and irresponsibility. Remember to take the time to learn from past mistakes. The 5 usually calls for some degree of freedom and independence, so this would not be the best time to tie yourself down either personally or professionally. New experiences and travel are possible. This is an excellent time to express creativity and innovation in your work or business.

6 Pinnacle

A 6 Pinnacle is often a time when relationships and family life become important. Many people settle down and try to establish balance in their lives in a 6 Pinnacle. You may want to bring some romance back into your relationship or spend more time with children and friends. Unresolved relationship issues can come to a head. If you have many 6s among your core numbers and have not yet established healthy boundaries between yourself and others, you could be doing far more than is necessary for others. You don't need to sacrifice yourself in order to be loved or appreciated. If you are lacking in 6 energy, you could become resentful of the demands made by others on your time and energy. Finding a balance of responsibility, support, companionship, and service to others will bring many rewards. You could enjoy working as a volunteer in a community or charitable organization. This may also be a good period to develop an artistic talent, and of course, this is an excellent time to use your management skills.

7 Pinnacle

During a 7 Pinnacle, and especially if it is a 16/7, you could feel a bit at odds with the general trends in the world around you. There is a sense of differentness, like a square peg trying to fit into round holes. This is a time of inner questioning, search, and spiritual exploration. This can be a challenging period for personal relationships as your focus is mostly inward. You may want to move away from the noise of the busy city. It is an excellent time for study, research, intellectual occupations, writing, solitary activity, meditation, and the inner life. It is important to guard against excessive feelings of specialness and even antisocial behaviour. Enjoy doing things alone, but avoid hiding in solitude. This is not likely to be the most sociable or outgoing period of your life. Instead, socialize with people who have similar interests to yours. Material accomplishment and money take a back seat. In fact, you may be inclined to flee the material world. Specialize, hone your skills, and develop an expertise in your field of interest.

8 Pinnacle

The 8 Pinnacle very often is a period during which significant progress is made in career, business, and financial matters. Success, money, rewards, and recognition are possible. Whatever your field of activity, you will have a pragmatic rather than emotional approach. You have vision, ambition, and the discipline and focus to achieve your goals. Reach for tangible goals and results. This is a power period. This is an excellent time for developing business, organizational, and management skills. You develop a taste for personal success and material rewards. Guard against putting career before family, or money before people. Becoming overly materialistic or insensitive could cost you important relationships. Maintain a sense of balance, be realistic, and clarify your objectives. Even if your goals are more lofty than materialistic, hard work, confidence, and diligence will lead to the rewards you seek.

9 Pinnacle

During a 9 Pinnacle, attention should be channelled a bit away from personal interests, outward toward others, the community, or the welfare of humanity. When experienced as a First Pinnacle, a broad education should be considered. This is likely to be a time where you will be required to focus on the big picture, where a global approach rather than a personal or subjective approach will be most beneficial and productive. Compassion, open-mindedness, and understanding are necessary ingredients. This can be a period of high drama, where emotions run high and situations are experienced with great intensity. An important relationship, marriage, project, job, or other activity may come to an end, generating feelings of grief, or emptiness. Endings are necessary now as they will clear the way and allow you to move forward in the coming times. Travel, education, and large-scale undertakings are possible. Progress and success in business, the arts, and public life are favoured now.

An Inner Life Journey

The following personal account is included here as it clearly illustrates the power and effectiveness of deep visualization techniques when applied to concrete life circumstances. Despite the popularity of books that teach the power of mind and focusing on intention, many people remain under the misguided impression that meditation is for highly evolved spiritual beings, or that creative visualization is for gifted mystics and not for everyone. Granted, I had spent some years exploring various spiritual disciplines, but the technique described below, derived from these experiences, is very simple and easy to use and requires no particular training in meditation techniques. All that is required is a desire to experience change, a willingness to do something about your current circumstances, and the ability to sit quietly for brief periods of time.

The events described below occurred during a particularly challenging time, a transition period covering a 9 and a 1 Personal Year, as well as a transition from a 6 to a 1 Pinnacle. I was well into my 1 Personal Year when it occurred to me that it was time to take matters into my own hands and make some serious changes. Clearly, the number 1 energy was in full force. At the time, I lived in an apartment in the core of the city, surrounded by cement and asphalt, while I craved a garden and cedar hedge so badly it hurt inside. I was holding on to a job that I really didn't like, desperately afraid of not being able to survive if I pursued my true life purpose.

My fear of letting go and moving forward, something that should have been accomplished in the 9 Personal Year, was unmistakably symbolized by the post-infectious polyneuritis I had sustained following a losing battle with a flu virus the fall of that 9 Year. My body had become numb from the waist down to my toes. It no doubt sounds worse than it was; the condition didn't prevent me from walking or moving my legs, it only caused lack of sensation. The result was that I walked cautiously on spongy feet, and shaved my legs more slowly. It was, if anything, moderately annoying. I took this ailment as a symbol of my fear of walking on my true path.

The doctor had informed me, in a somewhat bland tone, that they didn't know everything about the workings of the spine and brain, and that the condition would probably remain permanent, a diagnosis that I found unacceptable having just turned 40. At the same time, I was struggling with early, probably stress-induced perimenopausal symptoms that included head-splitting migraines and a case of acne so severe that I would leave the apartment to shop for essentials in the evenings only, too embarrassed to be seen in the light of day. I took this particular symptom as a symbol of my reluctance to face my true self. And then there were the heart palpitations, which speak for themselves.

Having had my fill of setbacks and obstacles, I decided to take action, but first, I needed to look deep inside and see what was driving my life. In need of quick results, I modified an inner journey exercise I had learned years before, simplifying it to the bare essentials I felt would be appropriate for my current situation. I settled comfortably on my couch, legs crossed beneath me. I had made certain that I would not be disturbed, and the apartment was silent. A stick of Japanese temple incense and a candle burned nearby. Note that candles and incense are not a

CHAPTER 13 · THE PINNACLE NUMBERS

requirement for effective meditation. They simply happened to be part of the rituals I enjoyed for setting the mood.

With eyes closed, I focused my attention on the space behind my eyes, in the centre of my head. From there, I visualized an elevator, which I took for the journey down to my core, which I pictured at the level of my pelvic girdle. I then left the elevator and entered a cavern-like chamber. I looked around for objects that might give me clues as to what was influencing me at the level of my foundation. The cavern was empty. Good sign, I thought. No objects, no foreign influences. Then I proceeded to find the exit of the cavern, over to the front and toward the left slightly. I headed outside to explore my path in search of clues that might indicate why my life was so jammed up and what I might do to clear the way.

What a shock I experienced when I reached the start of my path! Normally, the path should be natural, like a footpath in the woods, clear of objects and people, for these are indicators of outside influences. Instead, what arose before me was literally the largest pile of garbage I had ever seen. It was as though refuse from the entire Island of Montreal had been dumped on my path. Shocked, but not surprised, I proceeded to take action. I understood that I had to consciously destroy all that was blocking my progress. I also knew that what lay on my path were my own unresolved issues, garbage from my life, matters I had not completely dealt with such as fear, insecurity, lack of confidence, and self-esteem issues.

Determined to clear the way, I strapped on the largest laser-firing bazooka I could imagine myself holding, and began to fire away. That's the fun part of creative visualization. You can allow yourself to imagine whatever works for you. Of course, I understood that it would take many excursions before the entire heap of waste was destroyed. Also, I would have to take measures in my physical life in parallel to actions taken in my imagined inner life. But I was optimistic. I had found something that spoke to me, and I was determined to deal with it. Which is exactly what I did.

The first order of business was to terminate a very toxic relationship. Afterward, I gathered my courage and negotiated a leave from my job that allowed me to work as a contractor while building my consulting practice on the side. I accidentally (if there are truly accidents) rediscovered the Bach Flower Remedies, when a book, jutting out of its shelf space at my local homeopathic pharmacy caught my attention. These remedies, which I had used during the Dark Night of the Soul period in my youth, helped take the edge off the deeper fears, insecurities, and lack of confidence.

Every once in a while, I would repeat the process, returning to my path, firing away additional rounds of ammunition. Month by month, the pile grew smaller and smaller. A little over a year later, nearly all physical symptoms had disappeared, including the polyneuritis. I cancelled my monthly appointments with the neurologist. I was also well on my way to building my consulting practice and I had purchased my first home, and, yes, it was surrounded by a cedar hedge and eventually had a large garden. A final journey to my inner self revealed a path that was clear of debris, made of soft fine golden sand, winding gently before me, clearly symbolic of the new life that was defining itself before me.

This technique served me well over the years, and also helped many of my clients clear blockages of their own. It is simple to use, and doesn't require tremendous visualization ability. It can also be lots of fun. There is no law that says that self-development and inner healing can't be enjoyable! For the discovery of this technique, I have to thank my 14/5 Life Path and Birth Day numbers. Sometimes impatience and the desire for change—in this case, healing—can be a good thing!

CHAPTER 14

Putting It All Together

Charting the 9-Year Epiycle

Now that you've acquired a taste for numbers, let's create a personal roadmap for easy yearly planning. When interpreting any of the numbers, always keep in mind the importance of putting the information into context. As we've already seen, age is a factor. What might appear to be challenging at one time in your life may be experienced as an opportunity at a later date. Also, your experience of the numbers is not static. You may express the energy of a number negatively in the early years, but with learning, growth, and improved self-awareness you will naturally progress to the positive expression of that same energy. Your experience of the numbers evolves as you grow, and by the same token, your understanding of the numbers will contribute to deeper self-knowledge. Learning about your numbers is a win-win situation!

Most of us can look back over our lives and recall periods that were in some way remarkable. There are difficult and challenging times, periods of insecurity, disappointment, loss, fear, and confusion. Then there are those happy, joyful, fulfilling, safe, and prosperous times, and other, sometimes lengthy periods that are entirely insignificant and forgettable. At any given moment, several cycles may be operating simultaneously, and it is the study of these cycles that will enable you to identify a particular trend or energy. A very helpful tool for short- and long-term planning is the 9-Year Epicycle Table. Don't worry; this step doesn't involve any calculations. The Epicycle Table consolidates your currently active numbers in an easy reference format.

As shown in Chapter 1, the numbers 1 through 9 trace out a sort of organic flow in the life experience, with each number adding an essential component to the growth and development of the next and eventually to the whole. The cycle begins with an initial burst of energy and a sense of renewal in the 1 Personal Year, builds to a peak in the 8 Personal Year of accomplishment, then winds down in the 9 Personal Year of completion and endings in preparation for the next 9-Year Epicycle. The more effectively you integrate the lessons and opportunities of the numbers encountered along the way, the more successful will be your experience of a particular period. For example, if you work hard at establishing healthy relationships in your 2 Personal Year, you are more likely to come across opportunities, or "lucky breaks," in your 3 Personal Year simply by knowing the right people in the right places.

Example 9-Year Epicycle for a person born June 29 1971									
Life Path 8; Pinnacle 6									
Personal Year	1	2	3	4	5	6	7	8	9
Year	2018	2019	2020	2021	2022	2023	2024	2025	2026
Age	47	48	49	50	51	52	53	54	55

In our example for a person born June 29, 1971, when combining the Personal Year numbers with the Pinnacles we can now map out a more comprehensive 9-Year Epicycle. From the table above, we can see that in 2025, this person is in an 8 Personal Year, (6 + 11 + 9 = 26; 2 + 6 = 8), at the peak of the current epicycle, and is approaching the end of the current epicycle. As the cycle peaks in 2025, in the 8 Personal Year, focus should be

CHAPTER 14 • PUTTING IT ALL TOGETHER

placed on bringing projects to completion. The following year, 2026, is a 9 Year of winding down. From the "Duration of the Pinnacles" Table in Chapter 13, we see that given the 8 Life Path, and the age of 54, this person is also in the 4th pinnacle, in this case, a number 6 (6 + 9 = 15; 1+5 = 6).

Exercise: Complete Your Current 9-Year Epicycle Chart

Having completed the calculations that relate to your Birth Date, you are now ready to put it all together and map out your journey. For a closer look at your current 9-Year Epicycle, complete the chart below. You will need the following numbers: Life Path (Chapter 2), Personal Year (Chapter 3), current pinnacle from the "Duration of the Pinnacles" Table, as well as the calendar years and ages associated with your current epicycle.

My Current 9-Year Epicycle									
Life Path:				Pinnacle:						
Personal Year	1	2	3	4	5	6	7	8	9
Year									
Age									

Charting the Long-Term Cycles

For a bigger picture of your journey, we can chart the Numbers as well as the starting dates and duration of the Pinnacles. In the example for the person with June 29, 1971 Birth Date, we see a number 8 Pinnacle in the early years of life, reinforcing the 8 Life Path. The Second Pinnacle, a number 2, likely brought some relationship learning opportunities. The Third Pinnacle, being a 1, brought the focus back to self. The Fourth Pinnacle, a 6, accentuated the need for balance between self and others, between personal goals, and the need to help make the journey smoother for others. These Pinnacles show an interesting push and pull between self-serving motivation and a sense of service and collaboration.

	1st Pinnacle	2nd Pinnacle	3rd Pinnacle	4th Pinnacle
Long-Term Cycles for a person born June 29, 1971, with an 8 Life Path				
Number	8	2	1	6
Start	1971	2000	2009	2018
Duration	36 - 8, 28 years	9 years	9 years	To end of life

Among the cycle changes, the Pinnacle changes are likely to signal the most significant turning points. Once the energy of the new Pinnacle has been engaged, the previous Pinnacle dissipates quickly. How you relate to a particular trend depends on a variety of factors. Not everyone responds in the same manner to the same situation. An avid skier will express great joy upon learning of a late March forecast of fresh snow, while an ardent gardener might bemoan the delay indicated by the same forecast. A period of 4 energy favouring hard work, structure, and organization might be a welcome trend for a forty-something businessperson working on establishing a solid plan for a new venture, while this same period might not be as welcome for the sixteen-year-old guided by raging hormones with nothing but partying on their mind. When judging upcoming trends, take your particular circumstances, including age, life experience, and degree of self-awareness, into consideration.

Exercise: Complete Your Long-Term Cycles Chart

For a final picture of your life's journey complete the chart below. Use the Pinnacle Numbers as well as the Start and Duration of the Pinnacles from the table in Chapter 13.

My Long-Term Cycles				
	1st Pinnacle	2nd Pinnacle	3rd Pinnacle	4th Pinnacle
Number				
Start				
Duration		9 years	9 years	To end of life

The Name Numbers

We've made it this far, how about introducing one more set of numbers? Your Birth Name can provide interesting additional information, as a numeric value is assigned to each letter. However, name numbers can be a little bit more complicated to work with. Not all alphabets have the same quantity of letters, so a translation to the English version of a name may require a modification of the original name, essentially changing its energetic or numeric signature. At times, spelling or other errors may occur when the name is officially registered. In certain cultures, names are modified to fit a religious protocol, as is the case where I was born in Quebec, Canada. Here, every girl had the name Marie added to her name, and every boy had the name Joseph added to his name, thus changing the name intended by the parent.

Still, without going into too much detail, we can gather some interesting information from the Birth Name. Refer to the keywords in Chapter 1 for the meaning of the numbers. Then simply apply these to the letters. These numbers may amplify a particular skill set, or help correct an imbalance of energy from the Birth Date numbers. You will find the values of the letters in the table below. Use these to calculate your Name numbers. Use the full name given to you by your parents, including middle name or names.

1	2	3	4	5	6	7	8	9
A	B	C	D	E	F	G	H	I
J	K	L	M	N	O	P	Q	R
S	T	U	V	W	X	Y	Z	

Example Name numbers for Taylor Lee Parker:

Example: Taylor Lee Parker								
1	2	3	4	5	6	7	8	9
A	T	L		E	O	Y		R
A	K	L		E		P		R
				E				R
2	2	2	0	3	1	2	0	3

Place the letters of your name in the following table. The order of the numbers is not important for this exercise. Does one particular number stand out? The absence of a number can also stand out, especially if it is lacking in your Birth Day numbers. On the other hand, maybe you have a few number 3s in your name, but none in your Birth Date. You may have wondered where you got your talent for creative self-expression. Sometimes, a Life Path number can be strengthened many times over with repeated letters. For example, someone with a 4 Life Path and five Ds in their name will be very much marked by the number 4!

CHAPTER 14 • PUTTING IT ALL TOGETHER

Your Name:								
1	2	3	4	5	6	7	8	9

Should I Change My Name?

That's a good question, one for which there is not a simple "yes" or "no" answer. The name given at birth reflects the inner blueprint that will be the foundation for the life experience. It shows where balance is needed, what lessons can be learned; it brings out those unique skills that can be developed, but also any traumas or wounds brought in from past lives that are in need of healing.

Pay attention to all of your numbers, as your soul has very likely brought you the appropriate energy signatures needed for your growth in this lifetime. A name chosen later in life does not alter the basic profile. However, it may reflect those changes you have been working on. Once the lessons have been learned, you are free to rise above to an entirely different level of Being, one where the numbers, the astrology, or even your DNA do not matter.

Tips for Interpreting Your Numbers

- When completing your yearly planning and goal-setting, note any energies that might cause tension. For example, if you have a 7 Life Path and are currently experiencing a 2 Pinnacle and 6 Personal Year, you may find yourself pulled between a desire to tend to your own business (7) and the needs of coworkers, family, and friends (2 and 6). If you are not attentive, your relationships could suffer.
- Periods of tension can offer some of the greatest opportunities for learning and growth. They can be like the grains of sand that irritate the delicate lining of the oyster shell, causing it to secrete the nacre that will eventually turn the irritant into a pearl.
- Note the presence of High Energy and Master Numbers. These will indicate more intense lessons and experiences. Once their lessons have been learned, you can expect to manifest the greater potential of the number.
- Note the repetition of numbers, for example a 6 Personal Year with a 6 Life Path and a 6 Pinnacle. This may indicate a super-charged energy, making it difficult to manifest the number in a positive and balanced manner.
- Before making important decisions, consider your current epicycle. Are you at the beginning, middle, or end of your epicycle? This will help you refine your course of action. Early in a cycle, you might undertake new long-term projects; in the middle, you will want to focus on productivity, while at the end of an epicycle, you would want to bring projects to completion. If, for example, you have been inspired in a 5 Personal Year to take a completely new direction, keep in mind that in 4 years you will be experiencing a transition period. Ask yourself whether you are simply in need of a little freedom and adventure, as is often common in a 5 Year, or if the change is truly justified. If there is a change of Pinnacle

CHAPTER 14 • PUTTING IT ALL TOGETHER

number in your next cycle, you will likely be experiencing a change of focus, interest, and perhaps even job or career.
- When numbers change, be realistic in your expectations. Just because you are moving into an 8 Pinnacle, for example, it does not mean that you will become a financial mogul overnight. If you have no 8s among your numbers, you are typically not motivated by power, authority, money and business. The 8 Pinnacle might simply bring increased opportunities for material rewards, worldly recognition, or success.
- Look for patterns of numbers. The 2 and 6 combination usually indicates periods during which love and relationships are important, while 4s combined with 8s are more focused on business and money. When 3s, 6s, and 9s are found together, the arts and self-expression are important, while 1s and 5s focus on individuality and creativity. The 1s, 5s and 9s bring the most significant change, while 2s and 9s bring emotional situations and drama.

The numbers do not define you, and although they may show the general tone, purpose, and direction of your life journey, you remain free to navigate its waters. With the powerful and fascinating knowledge of your numbers, you will now be in a position to make the most appropriate choices given your personal trends. Above all else, use the numbers to make your journey fun, exciting, enriching, and rewarding.

Yearly Planning Made Better!

What can be better than all those amazing numbers we just put together? Well, how about adding two celestial cycles to the mix, no calculations needed! First, the Lunar Cycle, and second, Mercury Retrograde. Why add these? Because they have interesting and often very helpful correlations with our activities on Earth. For example, the Lunar Cycle can be very useful when planning certain activities, such as starting a new job or project, or putting a house up for sale. Then, knowing when Mercury is retrograde can help us better prepare for those periods of the year when communications might be problematic. So, let's put down our pencils and take a look up high, in the sky, for a change!

The Lunar Cycle

To keep it simple, we will focus on the waxing and waning phases of the Moon. The waxing Moon starts at the New Moon, or, as it is also known, the dark of the Moon. At this point in its 28-day cycle, the Moon, being between the Earth and the Sun, is not visible. The Moon then continues to move in its orbit around the Earth, every day growing in light, hence the term "waxing." After 2 weeks, it reaches the half-way point of its orbit, and is facing the Sun. It is now full. The second half of the lunar month is called the "waning" Moon phase. Over the next 2 weeks, the Moon diminishes in light, until it is no longer visible at the next New Moon. So, in effect, we have a 2-week period of growing light, and a 2-week period of diminishing light.

Where to find the New and Full Moon dates? Most agendas and calendars indicate these dates with a black dot for the New Moon and a white circle for the Full Moon. You can also find many online resources with dates for the yearly lunar cycles.

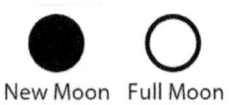

So, how can the lunar cycle be used in daily life? Let's say you want to start something that will have lasting effects, the best time to start is during the 2-week waxing Moon phase, that is, between the new and the full Moon. Whether you are starting a new job, a new project, a new relationship… anything with long-lasting potential, the best time to start is during this growing phase of the Moon. You are more likely to feel nurtured, inspired, and energetic during the waxing Moon phase, and so are more likely to lay down a solid foundation for future building.

CHAPTER 14 • PUTTING IT ALL TOGETHER

So, what can you do during the 2-week waning Moon phase? Appropriate activities for the waning Moon phase include working on existing projects, or even finishing off work that is in advanced stages. The energy is levelling off, so, work with what's at hand, clear the deck for new projects you will be undertaking during the next waxing Moon phase. Basically, it's time to take care of unfinished business. Learn from and integrate what you picked up during the waxing Moon phase. It is a time of appreciation for what you have.

The important point to keep in mind is that projects started during the waxing Moon phase are more likely to be sustained than those started during the waning Moon phase. Just as the sap goes up in the trees during the waxing Moon phase, the sap goes down to the roots during the waning Moon phase. Energy goes up during the building phase; energy goes down during the releasing phase.

How does the lunar cycle work with the sale or purchase of a home for example? Think waxing equals growing; waning equals diminishing. The desire to buy/sell grows during the waxing Moon phase, price remains high; the buyer is motivated and will pay a higher price. The desire to buy/sell diminishes during the waning Moon phase, the seller, tired of the process, can drop the price, but also, the buyer may lose interest. Being aware of these trends can give you an edge when buying or selling property. As a seller, you might plan your open house as the Full Moon approaches, when desire to purchase is at its strongest; as a buyer, you might make your offer during the waning Moon phase, when the price is more likely to drop, especially if the property was over-priced. Note that as a seller, if you want a fair price for your property, you might want to avoid home visits during the waning Moon phase, as your desire to stick to your price will "wane"; you may find yourself ready to sell at a lower price than you had originally intended.

Mercury Retrograde

Mercury has traditionally been associated with all things related to communications. When Mercury turns retrograde, we may encounter a higher than normal occurrence of issues in fields involving communications, from transportation to negotiations. Retrograde motion is the apparent backwards motion of a planet as it revolves around the Sun. It is akin to the optical illusion that occurs while riding in a car on the highway alongside a train. Due to variations in speed, the train appears at times to be moving backwards, relative to the speed of the car in which you are riding.

Mercury is retrograde approximately three times each year for 19-24 days. Typical Mercury Retrograde situations include: labour disruptions and strikes, rallies, marches, protests, breakdowns in negotiations, labour relations and peace talks, computer hardware and software problems and slowdowns, loss of mail, loss of luggage while travelling, car problems, delays in receiving mail and communications, loss of documents, mix-ups and errors in written and verbal communications.

When Mercury slows down and appears to reverse its course, it is a call to pay careful attention to all things involving communications. To ensure that your retrograde Mercury period goes smoothly, both personally and professionally, here are a few tips:

- Since the greatest level of intelligence is accessible while in a state of quiet peacefulness, try incorporating more meditation and quiet timeouts in your day. In the quiet mind, deeper learning, as well as greater awareness and insights, are possible.
- Reread important documents carefully, especially quotes and pricing for business transactions. All business, commercial, and financial documentation should be carefully edited and revised before signing and releasing.

CHAPTER 14 · PUTTING IT ALL TOGETHER

- Follow up on business communications, either with an email or telephone call. Avoid making assumptions. Confirm appointments before setting out for meetings. Bring a book or magazine to read if you expect to wait for an appointment.
- Give yourself ample time for mailing and shipping letters and packages. Now is not the time to take chances with important deadlines!
- If possible, postpone the signing of important documents such as leases, especially car leases, important sales orders and offers. If you must sign, reread carefully! Misplacing a "0" on a quote could spell disaster!
- Keep an eye on your luggage while travelling; keep your passport and important papers on your person.
- When on the road, pay attention to road signs and signals. Watch our for distracted drivers. No matter how good a driver you may be, if the other driver isn't paying attention, you could be in trouble. It's up to you to pay extra attention!
- Make sure your car is in top condition before going on a road trip.
- Clearly, this is not the best time to begin a new business venture. But if you must sign during this period, revise all contracts carefully. Otherwise, it is best to wait until Mercury returns to direct motion.
- Obviously, this is not the best time to purchase important communications equipment such as computers, phones, and automobiles! If you must make such a purchase during this time, obtain an outside, independent evaluation, and consider an extended guarantee.
- This cannot be said often enough: back up your important data, every day, more often if you are working on important documents! Keep your filing and paperwork up to date. It doesn't take much to lose your work!
- Do your due diligence! Take the time to think things through, do your homework, revise your plans as needed, and don't

be in a hurry to finalize important deals or matters, whether personal or business.
- This period is more favourable for introspection than for quick decision-making. Remember, don't rush, be still and check in with inner wisdom.
- This is a great time to engage in intensive study and research or pursue a subject in-depth.
- This is an excellent time to correct previous mistakes, especially those shopping errors you made just before Mercury turned retrograde. Don't be shy to return those mistaken purchases to the store!
- If all else fails, practise the gracious art of "not thinking" by going into the silence within, listening, paying attention and experiencing conscious awareness. You may be surprised at how good it feels to not think and try to figure things out!

When adding the Lunar Cycles and Mercury Retrograde periods to your Personal Year, you will have a clearer roadmap with which to plan the important events of your year. However, keep in mind that, in the end, it is not the numbers, the Lunar Cycles, or the retrograde motion of a planet that will determine your life. *You* determine your life, every moment of every day. You remain always free to choose how you will look, what you will see, and how you will proceed. Take charge of your journey, so you can make the best contribution for All! Thank You.

Bibliography

Campbell, Florence. *Your Days are Numbered*. Marina del Rey, CA: DeVorss & Company, 2002.

Christel, Alain-Victor. *Le Guide Pratique de la Nouvelle Numérologie*. Paris, France: De Vecchi Poche, 1989.

Cope, Lloyd. *The Astrologer's Forecasting Workbook*. Tempe, AZ: American Federation of Astrologers, 1995.

Covey, Stephen R. *The 7 Secrets of Highly Effective People*. New York: Fireside, 1990.

Decoz, Hans, and Tom Monte. *Numerology, Key to Your Inner Life*. New York: Perigee, 2002.

Edward, Pauline. *Astrological Crosses: Exploring the Cardinal, Fixed and Mutable Modes*. Montreal: Desert Lily Publications, 2013.

Goodwin, Matthew Oliver. *Numerology, The Complete Guide, Volume I*. North Hollywood, CA: Newcastle Publishing Company, 1981.

Goodwin, Matthew Oliver. *Numerology, The Complete Guide, Volume II*. North Hollywood, CA: Newcastle Publishing Company, 1981.

Tapiero, Martal A.O. *Les Nombres et le Destin*. Unpublished edition, 1979.

About the Author

Pauline Edward is an astrologer-numerologist, speaker, Certified Professional Coach and Group Leader. She is the recipient of a Chamber of Commerce Accolades Award for excellence in business practice. With a background in the sciences and a fascination for all things mystical, Pauline's journey has been enriched by a wide range of experiences from research in international economics, technical writing in R&D, and computer training, to studies in astrology, numerology, meditation, yoga, spirituality, shamanism, the Bach Flower Remedies, herbology, healing and reiki. Her profound desire to uncover the truth about the meaning of life was the inspiration behind her lifetime of writing. Now retired from consultation work, Pauline is available for speaking engagements and workshops. For information about upcoming events and publications, visit her website: http://www.paulineedward.com.

www.ingramcontent.com/pod-product-compliance
Lightning Source LLC
Chambersburg PA
CBHW070053080526
44586CB00013B/1035